THE LOCAL CHURCH:
God's Plan For Planet Earth

Jim Gent

ISBN 0-9640568-7-9
Library of Congress Catalog 94-065406

For information:

Smyrna Publications
P.O. Box 963
Old Bridge, New Jersey 08857

ii

What Preachers Have To Say About This Book!

"I was impressed with the content, format and practicality of the book. It bears all the marks of a scholarly, well-researched handbook with the advantage of readability. Some write to impress, some to inform. Thankfully you have chosen the latter. The wealth of quotes, illustrations, categorized scriptures and usable outlines qualify the book to be used as a Bible College text, a foundation for Sunday evening messages or Sunday School lessons."

Milton Ker, Pastor
Gospel Light Baptist Church, Lithia Springs, GA

"I have reviewed your study *The Local Church: God's Plan For Planet Earth* and sincerely appreciate the Biblical truths that you have brought out. These are things that every fundamental Baptist pastor needs to know, and you have so compiled the information that you have placed it at their fingertips. This would be an excellent study for missionaries to use on foreign fields in the establishment of their churches. It would also be excellent for new member's classes in local churches here at home. I sincerely appreciate the work that you have done. I hope you will do more with this publication by having it put into print and making it available to God's men everywhere."

Dr. Fred Mann, Pastor
Breezy Hill Baptist Church, Graniteville, SC

"Jim Gent certainly has the proper credentials for writing a book about the ministry of the New Testament local church! Having started churches and having pastored them for 30 years makes him of great value in helping God's people understand the scope and ministry of what a local church ought to be as given in God's Word. You will read this book with great profit, I believe, and gain great insights about the grand task of getting out the Good News that has warmed this old cold world's heart for nearly 2,000 years!"

Dr. Leonard Willinger, Associate Pastor
Trinity Baptist Church, Jacksonville, FL

"I hope this book will experience wide distribution among new converts and those who need to develop stronger convictions regarding the local church and their relationship to it. It contains information that is timely, comprehensive, practical and Biblical to the core! The message and materials contained in this volume will serve as a valuable tool for preachers, teachers and lay people alike."

Dr. Harry Vickery, Pastor
Heritage Baptist Community Church, Saddle Brook, NJ

"I appreciate your heart for the church which is evident in the book. New converts will get off on the right foot if these truths are engrafted into their lives immediately."

Bruce M. Humbert, Pastor
Saulk Trail Baptist Temple, Richton Park, IL

"I read your book and think it is really good. It is urgently needed as the Local Church is a forgotten doctrine. It is practical, scriptural, and challenging. It is not just facts, but it has heart."

Dr. Gary Gilmore, Evangelist
South Bend, IN

"I think it is a good work, and I am sure it would be very helpful."

Norman Pyle, Pastor
Bible Baptist Church, Riverdale, GA

"I was impressed with the thorough documentation and the value it will be to new Christians. The illustrations included add to its readability; I much enjoyed reading it."

Dr. Hal Webb, Evangelist
Conklin, NY

"The other evening, as a guest in Brother Gent's home, I requested his sharing with me the manuscript *The Local Church: God's Plan For Planet Earth*. I began to read page after page...how was I going to get any sleep? What a thrill for me to 'come alive' in the late night-early morning hours, as I raced through page after page. This is fantastic! I said to myself. This is what every pastor has to read! Brother

Gent says it right. It's all here in this fresh, fruitful, fulfilling book.

The theme of the local church has been neglected, *almost forgotten*. In this day, in this very hour men seek to do the work of God. They strive to fulfill the grandest and most glorious commission to go into all the world and preach the glorious gospel; often, they're choosing to fulfill His command by *their* methods. They energetically pursue personnel and purse from local fundamental churches, but they abhor any control of the local church in their own organizations! The local church is often bypassed by Christian leaders as they hastily pursue *their* own agenda. It is time to stop and examine our program. Are we in tune with the will of God to do the work of God through the Word of God? Are we working through the local church?

Abandon any 'ministry' whose grand goal is not the establishing and enlarging of the ministry of the local church.

You'll not read far into this book before you will have determined to teach this excellent material to your deacons and all of your workers.

I hasten to add that there is a group in your church who need this teaching more than any other. 'Who?' you may ask 'Whom?' Beloved pastor, your young people: your junior high, your senior high, your collegians. If they are neglected, if they are omitted in the teaching of this truth of the local church, it is highly possible they will be lost to the present and future ministry of your church and the Biblical work of the Lord.

Brother pastor, may I make a suggestion: switch Sunday School classes for at least a quarter. Teach these eternal truths yourself to your most valuable members: your own precious, priceless young people."

John Crabbe, Missionary Encourager
Fonda, NY

Contents

Contents

This book is about the local church: God's plan and program to carry on His work in this world. Certainly, God has a wonderful plan and program for the family; He also has a definite program for civil government; however, He has no other plan or program to carry on His work in this world apart from His church.

This volume is an "in the trenches" type book, written by a busy pastor wearing many hats. No claim is made for literary excellence. It is simply written by an active preacher, who has staunch Bible convictions about what he is writing, and is simply saying some things that he believes need to be said.

This is not a complex theological treatise; it is written for the everyday average Christian. It is not exhaustive; it simply withdraws a bucket from the vast ocean of God's informative revelation about His church.

It is my prayer that this book will: *help* new converts get headed in the right direction, *stimulate* believers to realize the primacy of the church, *foster* Biblical thinking among Christian High School and Bible College students about the importance of the local church, and *incite* Bible-teaching and Bible-preaching about "the pillar and ground of the truth."

To assist believers in getting a Biblical view of the church by stepping aside and letting *the Bible speak* is my objective.

PART I
LOCAL CHURCH
CHARACTERISTICS

1
New Testament Church Members Were Saved
(they knew they were forgiven)

---

*"... but thou art a God **ready to pardon** ..."*
(Nehemiah 9:17)

*"Come now let us reason together, saith the Lord: though your sins be as scarlet, they shall be as **white as snow** ..."*
(Isaiah 1:18)

*"Let the wicked forsake his way, and the unrighteous man his thoughts: and let him return unto the Lord, and he will have mercy upon him; and to our God, for he will **abundantly pardon**."*
(Isaiah 55:7)

"... thy sins are forgiven."
(Luke 7:48)

"And their sins and iniquities will I remember no more."
(Hebrews 10:17)

All the members of the New Testament Church were saved. They knew they were forgiven of all their sins. When Peter preached to Cornelius, who became the first Gentile convert, he preached unto him the forgiveness of sins through Jesus Christ. Acts 10:43 *"To him give all the prophets witness, that through his name whosoever*

1

believeth in him ***shall receive the remission of sins.***" Paul, preaching in the Galatian cities, preached the forgiveness of sins: *"Be it known unto you therefore, men and brethren, that through this man is preached unto you* ***the forgiveness of sins . . .***" (Acts 13:38).

THE PRESSING NEED

The Bible certainly teaches the pressing need for everyone to be forgiven of their sins. We all need to be forgiven because we are hopeless and helpless sinners. The Bible is crystal clear about this matter. *"For all have sinned and come short of the glory of God"* (Romans 3:23) is God's evaluation of everyone. The Bible does not teach that everyone has sinned in exactly the same way; however, the Bible does teach that we are all sinners.

A PRICELESS BLESSING

Forgiveness is a priceless blessing; it cannot be bought. All the money in the world cannot buy it. We can only be forgiven on the basis of the blood of Jesus Christ. Matthew 26:28 *"for this is my blood of the New Testament which is shed for many for* ***the remission of sins.***" Ephesians 1:7 *". . . Through his blood* ***the forgiveness of sins . . .***" The basis of forgiveness is the blood of Jesus Christ. Jesus Christ died on the cross in order that we might be forgiven of all our sins.

> I saw One hanging on a tree
> In agony and blood;
> He fixed His languid eyes on me
> As near His cross I stood.
>
> Sure, never, till my latest breath,
> Can I forget that look:
> It seemed to charge me with His death,
> Tho' not a word He spoke.

My conscience felt and owned the guilt,
And plunged me in despair;
I saw my sins His blood had spilt
And helped to nail Him there.

Alas! I knew not what I did –
But now my tears are vain:
Where shall my trembling soul be hid?
For I the Lord have slain.

A second look He gave, which said,
"I freely all forgive:
this blood is for thy ransom paid,
I die that thou may'st live."

Oh, can it be, upon a tree
The Savior died for me?
My soul is thrilled, my heart is filled,
To think He died for me.
                                    – John Newton

The story of George Wilson further illustrates this important truth. In 1829, a railway mail clerk named George Wilson killed his fellow clerk. He then stole the mail and tied himself in some way with a rope. When the train arrived at its destination they found Wilson tied up, and the dead clerk lying in his own blood. Wilson said that he had been assailed by bandits. But as the officers of the law began to question him, they found some discrepancies in his story. Wilson finally confessed that he had killed his partner and perpetrated the hoax. He was tried and sentenced to be hanged in the federal penitentiary. But as time passed, people seemed to forget the dastardly act and the sorrow of the dead man's family. Political pressure was brought upon President Andrew Jackson to pardon him.

The warden of the penitentiary told Wilson that the President of the United States had pardoned him. But, to the astonishment of the warden, George Wilson refused to accept the pardon. He wanted to be hanged. The warden did not know what to do. He called in the greatest legal minds, and the case was finally sent to the Supreme Court of the United States. The decision written by Chief Justice Marshall was handed down:

> "A pardon is a paper, the value of which depends upon its acceptance by the person to whom it is issued. It is hardly to be supposed that one under the sentence of death would refuse to accept a pardon, but if it is refused, it is no pardon. George Wilson must be hanged."

In the federal penitentiary at Leavenworth, Kansas, George Wilson was hanged.

The forgiveness that Jesus Christ freely offers only becomes effective in our lives when we accept Him as our personal Saviour.

A PRIMARY BLESSING

The forgiveness of sins through faith in the blood of Jesus Christ is one of the elementary, basic, and primary truths of the Bible. Could it be stated any clearer than Luke 24:47 *". . . and that repentance and remission of sins should be preached in his name among all nations . . ."* That is what Jesus told His followers to proclaim. The basic message of Bible preachers, according to Jesus, is the message of the forgiveness of sins.

A PERSONAL BLESSING

We can really know that our sins are forgiven through trusting Jesus Christ as our personal Saviour. Jesus said in Luke 7:48 *". . . thy sins are forgiven."* He wants to do the same for all of us today. Jesus' desire to forgive is the same today as it was then.

A Prompt Blessing

God longs to forgive us right now. Psalm 86:5 *"For thou, Lord, art good, and **ready to forgive**; and plenteous in mercy unto all them that call upon thee."* The Lord longs to forgive. Just as the father of the prodigal son was anxious to welcome his erring son when he returned. God can, will, and wants to forgive you right now if you realize you are a sinner in need of forgiveness and trust Jesus Christ as your personal Saviour.

The story is told of a godly widow who years ago lived in one of the great cities of Scotland. This godly widow's daughter came to her one day and said she was leaving home and did not want to follow the Christian ways of her mother. In spite of the fact that she was breaking the heart of her mother, the rebellious daughter left home.

For years the mother wept much. She earnestly prayed for her wayward daughter and longed so for her to return home. After much thought, she got the idea to take some of the pictures she had of her daughter and place them in various places around the city. Written at the bottom each picture in the mother's own handwriting was the message: **I LOVE YOU, PLEASE COME HOME**. She placed the pictures, among other places, in both of the rescue missions in the town. As time passed, and providence would have it, the daughter stumbled into one of the rescue missions. She saw her picture and read the words below it, **I LOVE YOU, PLEASE COME HOME**. Immediately her heart was pierced.

After the service she headed straight for home. In the wee hours of the morning, she finally arrived home. To her surprise, as she began to knock on the door, the door immediately opened. Because of the open door, she hurriedly ran to her mother's room thinking that

5

someone must have broken into the house and was possibly seeking to harm her mother. Awakening her mother, in tears she asked her mother if anyone had broken into the house. The mother thought she was dreaming, her daughter had finally arrived home; her prayers were answered. With tears in her eyes the mother replied: "Since the day you left, the door has never been locked; it has always been unlocked, hopefully awaiting your return." Spiritually speaking, we can say that God's love is much greater than the love of a mother for her daughter, and we can certainly say the door of God's forgiveness is always open! It is open this very moment for you to enter into the blessedness of God's amazing glorious **forgiveness**.

> O for the wonderful love He has promised,
> Promised for you and for me;
> Tho' we have sinned He has mercy and **pardon**,
> Pardon for you and for me.
>
> Come home, come home,
> Ye who are weary, come home;
> Earnestly, tenderly, Jesus is calling,
> Calling, "O sinner, come home!"
>   – Will L. Thompson

2

New Testament Church Members Were Baptized

(they were all immersed)

"Then they that gladly received his word were baptized . . ."
(Acts 2:41)

"And Crispus, the chief ruler of the synagogue, believed on the Lord with all his house; and many of the Corinthians hearing believed, and were baptized."
(Acts 18:8)

All the questions we have about baptism are clearly answered in the New Testament. The Scriptures tell us: how, who, why, and when we should be baptized.

How? "BAPTIZO"

The word baptize means to dip or **immerse**. Fifty reputable authoritative Greek lexicons (dictionaries) give **immersion** as the basic meaning of the Greek word **baptizo**.[1] The Bible way to be baptized is by **immersion**.[2]

John Calvin said "The very word baptizo means to **immerse**. It is certain that **immersion** was the practice of the early church."[3] Martin Luther stated a similar thought when he said: "Baptize is a Greek word and may be translated **immersion**. I would have those who are baptized, wholly dipped in water."[4] The testimony of John Wesley is clear: "Buried with Him in baptism alluding to the ancient method of **immersion**."[5]

Only believers are to be baptized. According to the subsequent verses, only those who have been saved are to be baptized.

Acts 2:41 – *"Then they that gladly received his word were baptized: and the same day there were added unto them about three thousand souls."*

Acts 8:12 – *"But when they believed Philip preaching the things concerning the kingdom of God, and the name of Jesus Christ, they were baptized, both men and women."*

Acts 8:36-38 – *"And as they went on their way, they came unto a certain water: and the eunuch said, See, here is water; what doth hinder me to be baptized? And Philip said, If thou believest with all thine heart, thou mayest. And he answered and said, I believe that Jesus Christ is the Son of God. And he commanded the chariot to stand still: and they went down both into the water, both Philip and the eunuch; and he baptized him."*

Acts 10:47 – *"Can any man forbid water, that these should not be baptized, which have received the Holy Ghost as well as we?"*

Acts 18:8 – *"And Crispus, the chief ruler of the synagogue, believed on the Lord with all his house; and many of the Corinthians hearing believed, and were baptized."*

Jesus made it clear in Matthew 28:19, only those who are His followers are to be baptized. Only saved people are to be baptized. In the Bible, **baptism is always subsequent to salvation and never precedes salvation**.

The Bible knows nothing of infant baptism or anyone being baptized before they are saved. There are many evil effects of infant baptism: (1) infant baptism prevents obedience to Christ's command (Acts 8:36, 37); (2) infant baptism leads to ceremonial salvation; (3) infant baptism puts tradition above the Bible.

Only believers are to be baptized.

WHY? OBEDIENCE

We are commanded by the Master, the Lord Jesus Christ, to be baptized. Jesus gave the command in Matthew 28:19, 20. Therefore, we ought to obey this divine command that was given to us by the Lord Himself! Another good reason is to follow the example that is clearly laid down in the New Testament: Acts 2:41; 8:13; 8:36-38; 16:32, 33; 19:5. To let people know you really want to live for Christ is another good reason (Romans 6:2-4).

Baptism was the way a saved person became identified with the local church. Acts 2:41 *"And they that gladly received the word were baptized and the same day there were added unto them about three thousand souls."* **All New Testament Church Members were immersed**.

WHEN? AS SOON AS POSSIBLE, AFTER YOU ARE SAVED

Cornelius, the Ethiopian, and the Philippian jailor, were all baptized as soon after they were saved as possible. Check it out in Acts 8, 10, and 16. The pattern is clear, believers' baptism was the first step of Christian obedience (Acts 2:41; 8:36-38).

According to the Word of God, all New Testament Church Members were immersed as soon as possible after they were saved. There is no other standard or pattern in the New Testament.

3

New Testament Church Members Faithfully Observed The Lord's Supper

(it was not an option)

"And when he had given thanks, he brake it, and said, Take, eat: this is my body, which is broken for you: this do in remembrance of me. After the same manner also he took the cup, when he had supped, saying, This cup is the new testament in my blood: this do ye, as oft as ye drink it, in remembrance of me. For as often as ye eat this bread and drink this cup, ye do show the Lord's death till he come."
(I Corinthians 11:24-26)

Some churches call the Lord's Supper (communion) a sacrament. We do not use the word sacrament when referring to the Lord's Supper because the word sacrament denotes an imparting of grace which obtains salvation. The word we commonly use in describing the Lord's Supper is ordinance. We refer to two church ordinances: Believer's Baptism and the Lord's Supper. Both Believer's Baptism and the Lord's Supper are commanded in the scriptures to be practiced by believers; they were observed in the New Testament Church; and neither of them have any saving power. However, they are to be observed by believers today in keeping with the New Testament.

When a believer follows the scriptural teaching in this area it always brings blessing and benefit and leads to **a closer and deeper walk with Christ.**

"This do in remembrance of me." The Lord's Supper is: (1) a memorial, (2) a symbol, and (3) a means of spiritual edification.

THE ESTABLISHMENT OF THE LORD'S SUPPER

Jesus commanded His disciples to participate in the Lord's Supper (Matthew 26:26). It was clearly recognized as a command to be followed by the early church (I Corinthians 11:26). This command is in effect until the Second Coming of Jesus Christ (I Corinthians 11:26).

THE MEANING

It should be strongly emphasized that the bread and fruit of the vine are **symbols** and merely picture to us the body and blood of Christ. Fundamentally, the Lord's Supper is a memorial to the death of Jesus Christ (I Corinthians 11:26). It is a reminder, a memorial, of His body: the bread (I Corinthians 11:24), and His blood: the cup (I Corinthians 11:25).

A REMINDER

First, the Lord's Supper reminds us to examine ourselves (I Corinthians 11:28-31). **Second**, it reminds us to confess our sins (I Corinthians 11:31). **Third**, the Lord's Supper is a gracious reminder that we have complete cleansing as a Christian through the precious blood of Jesus Christ (Matthew 26:26-28). **Finally**, it reminds us to be fully obedient to Christ because He was fully obedient at all times in His body while upon earth (I Corinthians 11:24).

Sad to say, many believers look upon the Lord's Supper as an option, a take it or leave it matter. According to the New Testament, the Lord's Supper was faithfully observed by the believers in the early church. It was not an option! We are to faithfully and systematically observe it until Jesus comes again (I Corinthians 11:26). No one is in a New Testament Church unless he is consistently given the opportunity to observe the Lord's Supper.

Many times a church's doctrinal soundness is directly related to what they believe about the Lord's Supper. It is a good indicator as to where a church stands on various doctrinal issues.

A SAFEGUARD AGAINST BACKSLIDING

It is difficult to Biblically and systematically observe the Lord's Supper and remain in a backslidden condition. The Lord's Supper will help any Christian be a better Christian.

No believer ever, under any circumstance, outgrows his need for the Lord's Supper.

4

The New Testament Church Was A Praying Church
(they really prayed!)

". . . but prayer was made without ceasing of the church unto God . . ."
(Acts 12:5)

The Bible clearly indicates that the early church was a praying church. No question about it.

I Didn't Realize The Book Of Acts Had So Much To Say About Prayer

Acts 1:14 – *"These all continued with one accord in* **prayer** *and supplication . . ."*

Acts 1:24 – *"And they* **prayed** *. . ."*

Acts 4:31 – *"And when they had* **prayed***, the place was shaken where they were assembled together; and they were all filled with the Holy Ghost, and they spake the word of God with boldness."*

Acts 6:4 – *"But we will give ourselves continually to* **prayer***, and to the ministry of the word."*

Acts 6:6 – *". . . and when they had* **prayed** *. . ."*

Acts 8:15 – *"Who when they were come down,* **prayed** *for them . . ."*

15

Acts 9:40 – *"But Peter put them all forth, and kneeled down, and* **prayed** . . ."

Acts 10:2 – *". . . and* **prayed** *to God alway . . .",* verse 30 – *"And Cornelius said, Four days ago I was fasting until this hour: and at the ninth hour I* **prayed** *in my house . . .",* verse 31, *"And said, Cornelius, thy* **prayer** *is heard . . ."*

Acts 12:5 – *"Peter therefore was kept in prison: but* **prayer** *was made without ceasing of the church unto God for him."*

Acts 13:3 – *"And when they had fasted and* **prayed** . . ."

Acts 14:23 – "And when they had ordained them elders in every church, and had **prayed** *with fasting, they commended them to the Lord, on whom they believed."*

Acts 16:13 – *"And on the Sabbath we went out of the city by a river side, where* **prayer** *was wont to be made . . ."*

Acts 16:25 – *"And at midnight Paul and Silas* **prayed***, and sang praises unto God . . ."*

Acts 20:36 – *"And when he had thus spoken, we kneeled down, and* **prayed** *with them all."*

Acts 21:5 – *". . . And we kneeled down on the shore, and* **prayed***."*

Acts 22:17 – *". . . while I* **prayed** . . ."

Acts 28:8 – *". . . to whom Paul entered in, and* **prayed***."*

The New Testament Church Was A Praying Church

THE LEADERS WERE MEN OF PRAYER

It is said of the early church leaders in Acts 6:4 – *"But we will give ourselves continually to **prayer** . . ."*

Paul said in Colossians 1:3 – *". . . **praying** always for you."* It is said of Epaphras in Colossians 4:12, *"Epaphras, who is one of you, a servant of Christ, saluteth you, always labouring fervently for you in **prayers** . . ."*

What a challenging verse is found in I Thessalonians 3:10 – *"Night and day **praying** exceedingly . . ."*

The leaders in the early church were men of prayer.

THE BELIEVERS WERE
CONSTANTLY ENCOURAGED TO PRAY

Romans 15:30 – *"Now I beseech you, brethren, for the Lord Jesus Christ's sake, and for the love of the Spirit, that ye strive together with me in your **prayers** to God for me."*

II Corinthians 1:11 – *"Ye also helping together by **prayer** for us . . ."*

In Ephesians 6:19 Paul requested believers to **pray** for him – *"And for me that utterance may be given unto me, that I may open my mouth boldly, to make known the mystery of the Gospel"* (Ephesians 6:19).

In Philippians 1:19 we see that Paul depended heavily upon the prayers of believers – *"For I know that this shall turn to my salvation through your **prayer** . . ."*

Colossians 4:3 – *"Withal **praying** also for us, that God would . . ."*

I Thessalonians 5:25 – *"Brethren **pray** for us."*

II Thessalonians 3:1– *"Finally, brethren **pray** for us that the word of the Lord may have free course, and be glorified even as it is with you."*

Paul's confidence in prayer is noted in Philemon 22 – *". . . for I trust through your **prayers** I shall be given unto you."*

I Thessalonians 5:17 – *"**Pray** without ceasing."*

PRAYER: THE KEY TO GOD'S BLESSING IN THE CHURCH!

How much more of the true blessing of God would we enjoy if we only got serious with God in prayer? We commonly look upon prayer as a spice. We sprinkle our prayers here and there. In the early church, prayer was the main ingredient.

5

New Testament Church Members Were Pure
(living clean in a dirty world)

". . . glorify God in your body . . ."
(I Corinthians 6:20)

In I Corinthians 5, Paul exhorts the church - *"put away from among yourselves that wicked person,"* specifically referring to someone practicing sexual immorality.

In I Thessalonians 4, Paul gives seven reasons why a believer should live a life of purity.

SEVEN REASONS FOR PURITY

An outline of the book of I Thessalonians that revolves around the word model is as follows: Chapter 1 – Model Evangelism; Chapter 2 – Model Servant ; Chapter 3 – Model Follow-Up; Chapter 4:1- 5:11 – Model Walk; Chapter 5:12-23 – Model Church Member. In Chapter 4:1 through 5:11, we have the model walk of the child of God, in this section in 4:3-8, Paul states seven reasons why a believer should be morally pure in a society in which immorality and illicit sex was rampant, common, widespread, and socially accepted. (Who says the Bible is not relevant for today!)

First, it is God's will to be pure and virtuous (4:3, 7). Referring specifically about moral purity Paul states, *"For this is the will of God, even your sanctification, that ye should abstain from fornication."* The Bible does specifically teach abstinence from sex before marriage and outside of marriage. Abstinence is scriptural! Sex outside of marriage is sin. *"For God hath not called us unto uncleanness, but unto holiness"* (I Thessalonians 4:7). Purity is not only the will of God, but also, the calling of God for every believer. It is the plain, clear, undebatable, **will of God and calling of God** for all believers.

Second, a believer should control his body (4:4): *"That every one of you should know how to possess his vessel in sanctification and honor."* The word vessel refers to one's own body (II Corinthians 4:7; II Timothy 2:21). A believer should control his body to maintain its purity. That is exactly what Joseph did (Genesis 39:7-12), and that is what Paul exhorted Timothy to do (I Timothy 5:2).

Third, a believer is not to act like the unsaved (4:5) *"Not in the lust of concupiscence (passion of lust), even as the Gentiles which know not God."* Just because everyone is doing it doesn't make it right! A believer is to be different; he should not act like the unsaved.

Fourth, impurity is defrauding (4:6a) *"That no man go beyond and defraud his brother in any matter . . ."* *"go beyond"* the boundaries fixed by God, *"defraud"* taking that which belongs to another (stealing). It is wrong to steal a car, and it is also wrong to steal a wife! *"Thou shalt not covet thy neighbour's wife"* (Exodus 20:17) and many other similar verses are still in the Bible. Adultery and fornication is sin; sex outside of and before marriage is sin. According to I Corinthians 6:9, 10, neither fornicators nor adulterers shall inherit the kingdom of God. It is always wrong to steal someone's wife, and it is also always wrong to steal someone's purity. Cars and money can easily be given back; purity cannot.

Fifth, immorality is dangerous (4:6) *". . . because the Lord is the avenger of all such . . ."* The Word of God appeals here to the fear of the consequences. According to the Bible, there are physical (volumes could be written about this: venereal diseases, AIDS, etc., etc.), emotional, mental, and eternal consequences when a person is promiscuous. *"Whoremongers and adulterers God will judge"* (Hebrews 13:4).

Sixth, immorality is despiteful (4:8a) *"He therefore that despiseth, despiseth not man, but God . . ."* When a person lives an impure life, he is rejecting God. *"Thou shalt not commit adultery"* and many other similar verses are still in the Bible.

Seventh, a believer can live a morally pure life because he possesses the dynamic of the indwelling Holy Spirit (4:8b) *". . . who hath also given unto us his Holy Spirit."* This does not mean a person will not struggle with temptation; however, through the power of the Holy Spirit, Who indwells every believer, we can have victory. *"There hath no temptation taken you but such as is common to man: But God is faithful, who will not suffer you to be tempted above that ye are able; but will with the temptation also make a way to escape, that ye may be able to bear it"* (I Corinthians 10:13).

If there was ever a day in which we need to be on guard and alert in order that we will not have permissive attitudes concerning the dirty, profane, depraved, salacious, and shameless: television programs, music, magazines, movies, and dress styles, that encourage and promote unbiblical behavior, IT IS TODAY!

As we are in fellowship with Jesus Christ, thank God, we can be pure and clean in the midst of a dirty society.

A closing word to the unsaved: If you have really messed up your life in this specific area, Jesus Christ can straighten you out. Please read I Corinthians 6:9-11 *"And such **were** some of you: But ye are washed . . ."*

6

New Testament Church Members Were Separated

(why leave a liberal church?)

*"Wherefore come out from among them,
and be ye separate, saith the Lord . . ."*
(II Corinthians 6:17)

*"Let us go forth therefore unto him without
the camp . . ."*
(Hebrews 13:13)

*"Blessed is the man that walketh not in the
counsel of the ungodly . . ."*
(Psalm 1:1)

WHY LEAVE A LIBERAL CHURCH

REASON 1 – BECAUSE OF THE CLEAR TEACHING OF THE BIBLE. The local church is referred to about 100 times in the New Testament. It is clearly God's will for a believer to be identified with, not just any local church, but a Bible-believing, fundamental, New Testament church.

REASON 2 – OUR MONEY IS TO SUPPORT GOD'S WORK, NOT THE DEVIL'S. If a person is a member of a liberal or modernistic church, or a church that is not true to the Bible, that person is actually supporting the devil's program, according to II Corinthians 11:13-15. Certainly, it is not God's will for God's people to support the devil's program! However, many people are doing that very thing.

REASON 3 – THE BIBLE EMPHATICALLY TEACHES SEPARATION FROM RELIGIOUS HERESY. It is our God-given responsibility to separate from false doctrine. II John 7-11 and Romans 16:17 are clear even to the casual reader.

REASON 4 – BELIEVERS ARE NOT TO BE YOKED WITH UNBELIEVERS. God's people are to be kind and forgiving (Ephesians 4:32). However, when it comes to God's work, the Bible is plain and clear, believers are not to be united with unbelievers (II Corinthians 6:14).

REASON 5 – CHURCHES, RELIGIOUS ESTABLISHMENTS, AND DENOMINATIONS ARE NOT ALWAYS TRUE TO CHRIST. The religious establishment of Jesus' day thoroughly rejected Him (John 8:40, 44, 49, 55; Matthew 23:13, 33). There are several denominations today that are just as much in danger of the damnation of hell as the religious establishments of Jesus' day.

INFIDELS IN THE PULPIT . . .

In a survey made of 500 pastors, they were asked if they believed the Genesis account of creation: 47% said they did, 5% were uncertain and 48% did not!

The same question was asked of 200 theological students (future "preachers" of America): 5% said they did, 6% were uncertain, and 89% DID NOT!

Modern Churches Cool Toward Concept of Hell (Baby boomers believe in second, third, and fourth chances.) Newspaper article by Peggy Landers, Knight -Ridder Newspaper, November, 1993.

New Testament Church Members Were Separated

MANY CLERGYMEN DO NOT BELIEVE IN HELL .. . .

Mr. Warren Herring of the *News Free Press* in Chattanooga, Tennessee, wrote a very thought-provoking article entitled "What Has Happened to Hell?" In this article he asked three questions: (1) Is Hell a literal place of eternal punishment, and if so, why are preachers neglecting the subject? (2) Is Hell too controversial for the average preacher today? (3) Do congregations and parishioners squirm when preachers preach on Hell-fire and brimstone?

He went to a number of different congregations in the city of Chattanooga and put certain preachers on the spot as to what they believed about the place called Hell.

The first church this man visited was the Unitarian Universalist church pastored by a Rev. John Wilkerson. He asked, "Mr. Wilkerson, what do you believe about the doctrine of Hell?" He said, "Well, I think hell is a time of purification, I think it is a time of cleaning when all things that are offensive to God in our lives are cleansed. Then we will come back to the earth. We will be reincarnated."

He went to a second clergyman, Rabbi Lloyd Goldman. He asked the rabbi, "Rabbi, what do you believe about the place called Hell?" He said, "Well, Sir, I think it is a state of being. I think Hell is right here now. I believe Hell is on this earth."

Again Mr. Herring visited with Pastor H. H. Battle of the (E. Eighth St.) First Baptist Church. He said, "Sir, what do you believe about Hell?" He said, "Sir, I cannot accept the fact that Hell is a place. I believe Hell is where the absence of God is felt."

LUTHERANS . . .

"44% of Lutherans believe that salvation depends upon being sincere in whatever you believe." *A Christian Handbook of Vital Issues* (New Haven: Leader, 1973) p. 369.

Lutheran Sexuality Study Unveiled "Masturbation is healthy, the Bible supports homosexual unions, and teaching teens how to use condoms to prevent disease is a moral imperative, says a task force leading the nation's largest Lutheran body into the sex wars. Four years in the making, a draft statement going before the Evangelical Lutheran church in America declares that the core of human sexuality should be loving, committed relationships – and not limited to heterosexual marriages." *The Associated Press,* October 20, 1993.

UNITED METHODISTS . . .

This denomination does not have a single theological seminary that could be considered Bible-believing or even evangelical. *The Battle For The Bible* (Grand Rapids: Zondervan; 1976) p. 153.

It is informative to note that the United Methodists put reason, experience, and tradition on the same level as the Bible as sources of theological and doctrinal truth. *About Being United Methodists* (Greenfield: Bete; 1978), p. 5.

UNITED PRESBYTERIANS . . .

Scores of Presbyterian ministers do not believe the Bible to be trustworthy. *The Battle For the Bible* (Grand Rapids: Zondervan; 1976) pp. 149-152.

Episcopalians - Most U.S. Episcopalians (70%) say sexually active gays and lesbians still can be faithful Christians, according to a denomination-sponsored survey. The church polled nearly 20,000 members in 75 of 96 dioceses to gauge popular opinion for sexuality discussions in parishes. (1993)

REASON 6 – SOME CHURCHES ARE NOT ONLY UNBIBLICAL, BUT WICKED. Beer and Bingo are par for the course among scores of "religious people." Some churches are simply glorified Las Vegas joints!

A treasurer of a certain church told me that his minister receives a delivery of liquor from the local liquor store each Saturday night and charges it to the church!

INTERFAITH GROUP WELCOMES WITCH . . .

Pastor Ken Steigler, a Salem, Massachusetts, Methodist pastor withdrew from a local interfaith group last year because it welcomed into its ranks a witch! (1993)

REVOLUTION OR RELIGION . . .

"Do You Know Where Your Church Offerings Go? You'd Better Find Out, Because They May Be Supporting Revolution Instead of Religion" An eye opening article by Rafl Jean Isam in January, 1983, *Reader's Digest.*

HOMOSEXUAL ORDINATION UPHELD . . .

The highest court in the Presbyterian Church (U.S.A.) approved in November, 1993, the ordination of two homosexuals as deacons in the Central Presbyterian Church of Eugene, Oregon. The church ordained a homosexual man and a lesbian.

DENOMINATION OPENLY ORDAINS HOMOSEXUAL PRIESTS AND ABANDONS THE SCRIPTURES . . .

A suburban Chicago Episcopal Church (Church of the Resurrection, Rev. William Beasley) voted to leave the Episcopal Denomination because the denomination has openly ordained homosexual priests and has abandoned the Scriptures. (November, 1993)

UNBELIEVABLE . . .

The General Theological Seminary (Episcopal in New York City) is willing to make apartments available to committed same-sex couples according to its new campus housing policy. Trustees of the 150-student seminary changed the rules on January 10, 1994, in response to a tenured **lesbian professor's** complaint to the New York City Commission on Human Rights. She claimed the seminary discriminated against her and her domestic partner on the basis of sexual orientation.

HOMOSEXUALS AND LESBIANS BEING ORDAINED . . .

The new lesbian Episcopal priest who was recently ordained by Bishop Paul Moore in Manhattan had her picture in *Time Magazine.* "Barrett, who has been studying for a doctorate in social ethics at the Graduate Theological Union in Berkley, goes somewhat beyond 'homosexual tendencies.' She said candidly that her relationship with her lesbian lover is 'what feeds the strength and compassion I bring to the ministry.' She also believes that 'homosexuality is an alternative life style that can be a good and creative thing.'"

These deplorable things are commonly reported in our daily newspapers and news magazines.

I could go on and on and mention many other things. Actually, books could be written about this subject.

However, the point is obvious: there are innumberable ungodly things taking place in churches today.

REASON 7 – HEBREWS 13:12, 13 IS CLEAR. The writer to the Hebrews is exhorting the Hebrew Christians to make a clean break with Judaism. We might say, Judaism was the religious establishment of their day and the religion which these people were identified with before they were saved. The point the writer of Hebrews is making is that they should make a clean break with their former religious affiliation because it is not true to Christ. The application is obvious: we should make a clean break with any religion which is not true to Christ even if it is the church to which we belong. Being true to Christ means separating ourselves from religion that is not true to Him. We ought to be willing to endure reproach for Him.

A pastor in a liberal denomination mentioned that he knows he should withdraw from the liberal denomination of which he is a member and supporter. However, he said he would not do it because he could not keep his pension.

There are scores of people in liberal and modernistic churches because they are unwilling to bear reproach for Christ.

REASON 8 – WE CANNOT OBEY PROVERBS 22:6 IN A LIBERAL CHURCH. It is the responsibility of parents to make sure their children are in a Christ-honoring, Bible-believing, New Testament Church. Proverbs 22:6 cannot be obeyed in its entirety apart from a sound local church.

REASON 9 – ALTHOUGH DISOBEDIENCE IS COMMON, THAT DOESN'T MAKE IT RIGHT. While talking to a Gospel singer this subject came up. The singer made it a habit to "perform" in some outright liberal churches. His thinking was that in so doing he was not compromising his message. As I mentioned to him, "The question is not compromising your message, as I am sure you do not, but it is a question of endorsing and putting your stamp of approval upon a church that is not true to the Bible nor the Lord Jesus Christ." The singer's purpose was not to expose the liberal churches, but rather, to promote them and actually build them up and add people to them.

No singer or preacher or anybody else has a right to build up or promote that which the Bible condemns. It may be good for the pocketbook, but it is not good for the cause of Christ. In fact, this is why so many of God's people are totally confused about this subject. Sad to say, there has been a lot of disobedience in this area.

REASON 10 – FALSE DOCTRINE IS DEMONIC. One of the main thrusts of demons (Satan's helpers) is to promote false doctrine (I Timothy 4:1-2). Anyone who lends support to churches that are not true to the Bible is engaged, many times unknowingly, in actual support of the devil's program in this world.

Demons love to promote morality, religion, and false doctrine of one sort or another. (Never get the mistaken idea that the devil is only interested in **promoting** immorality. He is out to damn people to hell. One of his easiest ways to do this is through religion!) We must never forget that Satan and his demons love to appear as angels of light (II Corinthians 11:14). They also like to quote the Bible (Matthew 4). In fact, the most likely place to find a demon is behind a pulpit!

Any person who supports a church or pastor who advocates salvation by: good deeds, church membership, baptism, taking communion, sacraments, being good, sincerity, morality, etc., is supporting the devil's program in this world (I Timothy 4:1-2; II Corinthians 11:13-15).

Are you supporting and promoting the devil's program???

REASON 11 – IT IS THE RIGHT AND PROPER THING TO DO. Why leave a liberal or modernistic church or a church that is not true to the Bible and join a fundamental, Bible-believing, Christ-honoring, local New Testament Church? Because, in the light of Scripture, it is the right and proper thing to do.

7

New Testament Church Members Were Understanding

(the Christlike spirit was apparent)

". . . forgiving one another, even as God for Christ's sake hath forgiven you."
(Ephesians 4:32)

New Testament Church members were exhorted to be kind, tenderhearted, and forgiving towards one another, according to Ephesians 4:32 *"Be ye kind one to another, tenderhearted, forgiving one another, even as God for Christ's sake hath forgiven you."* Matthew Henry has the following to say about this verse: **"Be ye kind one to another."** This implies the principle of love in the heart, and the outward expression of it, in an affable, humble, courteous behavior. It becomes the disciples of Jesus to be kind one to another, as those who have learned, and would teach, the art of obliging. **Tenderhearted**, this is, merciful, and having a tender sense of the distress and sufferings of others, so as to be quickly moved to compassion and pity. **Forgiving one another.** Occasions of difference will happen among Christ's disciples; and therefore they must be placable, and ready to forgive, therein resembling God himself . . ."[1]

POSITIVE BIBLE PRINCIPLES

"LOVE ONE ANOTHER" (JOHN 13:34-35). The Scripture is plain and clear. Believers ought to love one another. According to this passage, it is a command.

"BE KIND ONE TO ANOTHER" (EPHESIANS 4:32; COLOSSIANS 3:13). Believers are not only to love one another, but they are also to be kind to one another.

"BE TENDERHEARTED TOWARD ONE ANOTHER" (EPHESIANS 4:32). God's people ought to be sympathetic toward each other. Church members ought to have real affection toward one another.

Why do you suppose Paul mentioned this? Could it be that God's people were not showing the concern they should have for one another? Are God's people really concerned about one another today as they should be?

"TARRY (WAIT) FOR ONE ANOTHER" (I CORINTHIANS 11:33). The principle here is that believers ought to exercise longsuffering toward one another. Is longsuffering among believers the rule or the exception?

"FORGIVE ONE ANOTHER" (EPHESIANS 4:32; COLOSSIANS 3:13). There is no such thing as a perfect Christian or a perfect church. The quicker one realizes this the better off he will be. The Bible teaches that believers ought to be great forgivers in relation to their fellow believers. This is a much neglected principle of Christian conduct. Some believers have never forgiven their fellow believers and hold unhealthy grudges. Some have held hard feelings and unforgiving spirits for years. All of this is in violation of the clear Bible principle *"forgive one another."*

ENCOURAGE ONE ANOTHER (I THESSALONIANS 5:11). This passage is talking about how we need to be a blessing to one another. How many believers are dedicated to the task of being a blessing to other believers?

"BEAR YE ONE ANOTHER'S BURDENS" (GALATIANS 6:2). To bear one another's burdens certainly takes for granted the matter of being genuinely interested in our fellow believers.

It is interesting to study the phrase *"one another"* in the New Testament. **1.** *we belong to one another* (Romans 12:5) **2.** *care for one another* (Romans 12:10) **3.** *love one another* (I Peter 1:22; I John 3:11, 23; 4:7, 11, 12; II John 5) **4.** *not to condemn one another* (Romans 14:13) **5.** *humble toward one another* (Romans 12:16) **6.** *build up one another* (Romans 14:19) **7.** *receive one another* (Romans 15:7) **8.** *counsel one another* (Romans 15:14) **9.** *be patient with one another* (I Corinthians 11:33) **10.** *equal fellowship with one another* (I Corinthians 12:25) **11.** *show affection to one another* (I Corinthians 16:20) **12.** *not to consume one another* (Galatians 5:26) **13.** *serve one another* (Galatians 5:13) **14.** *we are not to provoke one another* (Galatians 5:26) **15.** *we are members one of another* (Ephesians 4:24) **16.** *submit to one another* (Ephesians 5:21) **17.** *not to lie to one another* (Colossians 3:9) **18.** *forbear one another* (Colossians 3:13) **19.** *admonish one another* (Colossians 3:13) **20.** *pray for one another* (I Thessalonians 3:12) **21.** *comfort one another* (I Thessalonians 4:18) **22.** *edify one another* (I Thessalonians 5:11) **23.** *exhort one another* (Hebrews 10:24) **24.** *consider one another* (Hebrews 10:24) **25.** *confess our faults to one another* (James 5:16) **26.** *use hospitality with one another* (I Peter 4:9) **27.** *be subject to one another* (I Peter 5:5) **28.** *we are to have fellowship with one another* (I John 1:7).

NEGATIVE BIBLE PRINCIPLES

BELIEVERS ARE NOT TO BE VENGEFUL (ROMANS 12:19-21). This passage tells us we are not to avenge. We are not to retaliate: we are not to try to get even when someone has openly done us wrong. Verse 21 says, *"Be not overcome of evil, but overcome evil with good."*

STRIFE IS NOT FROM THE LORD (JAMES 3:14, 15). James tells us that bitter envying (sharp jealousy) and strife (contentiousness) is devilish. Bad attitudes, strife, discord, and fussing and feuding among believers is of the devil.

WE ARE NOT TO SPEAK EVIL OF ONE ANOTHER (JAMES 4:11). Simply stated, James is saying stop running one another down.

NOT TO GO TO COURT WITH FELLOW BELIEVERS (I CORINTHIANS 6). There is a tremendous principle of Christian conduct to be derived from this passage. Namely if a fellow believer has done you wrong it is better to suffer the wrong rather than ruining the testimony of the local church. Lenski says the following concerning this passage: "Simply to suffer the wrong, the injustice, or the injury does not occur to many Christians. The least they do is to set up a loud complaint and then continue complaining and ill will. To forgive at once and to forget so thoroughly as to make no complaint at any time, is an unknown ethical practice even to brethren who think they are well read in the Scriptures and rather advanced Christians. Of course, when Paul asks the Corinthians why they do not rather suffer wrong he in no way excuses those who actually do wrong, nor encourages them to continue their wrong doing."[2]

Sometimes when everything is said and done and finished the innocent party stands as guilty as the erring party because he did not express a Christlike attitude and spirit as he should have!

According to the Bible, there is no place for gossip, discord, or strife among believers. These things are not in keeping with Christian character and conduct.

THE SAD SITUATION IN MANY CHURCHES

Sad to say, Bible principles, concerning a believer's

conduct toward his fellow believers, are commonly and repeatedly violated. More harm is done to, and in, our churches in this way than in any other way! The trouble and sorrow that many sins have caused is minor compared to the trouble and sorrow that is caused through strife, discord, gossip, grumbling, criticism, contention, and fussing.

How we all need to learn the lesson of the interlocked antlers. In a monastery in Germany there may be seen two pairs of antlers interlocked. They were found in that position many years ago. The deer had been fighting and their antlers got jammed together and could not be separated. They died with locked horns. One historian has said, "I would like to take those horns into every house and school in the country." And should we not add, "And into every church."

Why is discord so present in our churches? One reason is because our depraved human nature constantly tends to break the unity that the Holy Spirit is seeking to produce. A second reason is that Satan knows the harm that disunity can do; therefore, he is actively working to break up Christian unity (James 3:14, 15).

God's work prospers when God's people are united in the work of the Lord. In the 13 chapters of Nehemiah, the great Old Testament book on building for God, we find that the words *"we"* and *"us"* are used no less than 66 times. Unity is essential if we are going to accomplish anything for the Lord. A great principle is also found in Acts 1:14 *"one accord."* Souls are won when God's people are of *"one accord."*

When unity is not present, we usually wind up fighting the wrong enemy. When General Stonewall Jackson heard his men cutting each other down over what strategy to use in the conflict, he interjected: "Remember,

37

gentlemen, the enemy is over there," pointing in the direction of the battle that was then raging.

WHAT SHOULD WE DO?

CONFESS OUR FAILURE (I JOHN 1:9). Just about everyone of God's children have been guilty of miserable failure at one time or another in this area. How we need to admit our sin.

MAKE RESTITUTION. Confession has to do with our fellowship with the Lord; restitution has to do with our testimony. The Bible teaches that we are under obligation to make anything right that is in our power to make right (Leviticus 6:4; Proverbs 6:31; Luke 19:8; Philemon 18, 19). Someone came to Gypsy Smith once and said, "I have no peace; I am so miserable." There was something that this person needed to make right in a practical way with someone else. Gypsy Smith said, "You will never have peace until you make the matter right that you know you need to make right!" Some believers will never have peace until they make some things right. If there is something you need to make right, if there is some area in which you need to make restitution, don't put it off until tomorrow; make it right as soon as possible.

ASK THE LORD TO GIVE US A SWEET SPIRIT. We need to ask the Lord to give us a sweet spirit as exemplified in the life of Joseph (Genesis 50:21). Thank the Lord, the Holy Spirit can produce in us the spirit of Joseph, the Christlike spirit, the spirit and attitude that we ought to have (Galatians 5:22).

8

New Testament Churches Had Spiritual Pastors and Supportive Deacons
(not everyone is qualified)

". . . to all the saints in Christ Jesus which are at Philippi, with the bishops and deacons."
(Philippians 1:1)

Spiritual pastors, supportive deacons, soul winning members, were three basic characteristics of the New Testament Church according to Acts 6.

SPIRITUAL PASTORS

The following three words describe the office of the pastor in the New Testament Church: pastor, bishop, elder. The word pastor means shepherd (Acts 20:28); the word bishop emphasizes the idea of an overseer of the church (I Peter 5:2); the word elder denotes the idea of a man's maturity in the things of the Lord (I Timothy 5:17).

First, we know the New Testament pastors were spiritual men because of Acts 6:4 *But we will give ourselves continually to prayer, and to the ministry of the word."* These early church leaders were great men of prayer and they were also mighty in the Scriptures.

Second, we know they were spiritual because of the qualifications laid down in I Timothy 3:1-7. In this passage we have several qualifications or character qualities that should be true of every pastor: **1.** desire *"If a man desire the office of a bishop, he desireth a good work."* (I Timothy 3:2) **2.** blamelessness *"A bishop then must be blameless."* (I Timothy 3:2) **3.** husband of one wife *"A bishop then must be . . . the husband of one wife."* (I Timothy 3:2) **4.** sober *"A bishop must be . . . sober."* (I Timothy 3:2) **5.** given to hospitality *"A bishop must be . . . given to hospitality."* (I Timothy 3:2) **6.** apt to teach *"A bishop then must be . . . apt to teach."* (I Timothy 3:2) **7.** not given to wine *"A bishop then must be . . . not given to wine."* (I Timothy 3:2-3) **8.** no striker *"A bishop then must be . . . no striker."* (I Timothy 3:2-3) **9.** not greedy of filthy lucre *"A bishop must be . . . not greedy of filthy lucre."* (I Timothy 3:2-3) **10.** one that ruleth well his own house *"A bishop then must be . . . one that ruleth well his own house."* (I Timothy 3:2-4) **11.** not a novice *"The bishop then must be . . . not a novice."* (I Timothy 3:2-6) **12.** of good report *"A bishop then must be . . . of good report."* (I Timothy 3:2-7).

Another list of qualifications is found in Titus 1:6-9.

Third, their duties attest that they were spiritual. Some of the duties and responsibilities of the pastor are as follows: **1.** shepherd (Acts 20:28; I Peter 5:2) **2.** teacher (Ephesians 4:11, 12) **3.** example (I Timothy 4:12) **4.** watchman (Hebrews 13:17) **5.** laborer in the Word and doctrine (I Timothy 5:17) **6.** leader (I Timothy 3:2, Titus 1:9, I Timothy 5:17).

Fourth, the principles that Peter mentions in I Peter 5:1-3, confirm that they were spiritual. The following principles are stated in this passage: **1.** he is to shepherd the flock: that probably includes feeding, leading, encouraging, discipling, and guarding the flock, **2.** he should have a willing heart, **3.** he should not serve for *"shameful gain"* vs. 2, this obviously applies to money, as well as: prestige, power, and promotion, **4.** he should not be lazy (ready mind), **5.** he is a leader, not a lord *"Neither as being lords over God's heritage"* vs. 3, *"God's heritage"* specifically refers to the flock of which he is the pastor, **6.** he is to be an example (vs. 3). (In this passage it is interesting to note that Peter was not the first Pope, he refers to himself in verse 1 *"who am also an elder."* He included himself among the church leaders he was exhorting.)

Fifth, they had to be spiritual because of the responsibilities that the church had to them. The churches responsibilities to their pastors are as follows: **1.** know (appreciate) him (I Thess. 5:12); **2.** esteem him (I Thess. 5:13); **3.** obey him (Heb. 13:17); **4.** honor him (financial remuneration) (I Tim. 5:17, 18; I Cor. 9:13, 14; Gal. 6:6); **5.** remember him (Heb. 13:7); **6.** salute him (Heb. 13:24).

Obviously, New Testament churches had spiritual pastors.

SUPPORTIVE DEACONS

In Acts 6:1-4, we learn about the genesis of the office of the deacons: *"And in those days, when the number of the disciples was multiplied, there arose a murmuring of the Grecians against the Hebrews, because their widows were neglected in the daily ministration* (distribution). *Then the twelve called the multitude of the disciples unto them, and said it is not reason that we should leave the word of God, and serve tables. Wherefore, brethren, look ye out among you seven men of honest report full of the Holy Ghost and wisdom, whom we may appoint over this business. But we will give ourselves continually to prayer and to the ministry of the word. And the saying pleased the whole multitude: and they chose Stephen, a man full of faith and the Holy Ghost, and Philip, the Prochorus, and Nicanor, and Timon, and Parmenas, and Nicholas a proselyte of Antioch: whom they set before the apostles . . ."*

The word "serve" in Acts 6:2 is the same as the word *"deacon"* in I Timothy 3:8. It is also used in John 2:5, *"servants,"* and in John 2:9, *"servants."* The word obviously means servant. Deacons are not to be in competition with the pastor; but rather, they are to be his helpers and servants. This is the clear meaning of the Acts 6 passage; they enabled him to spend more time in prayer and in the Word.

In I Timothy 3:8-13, the Word of God lays down fourteen qualifications, or character qualities, that should be true of every deacon. I Timothy 3:8-13 – *"Likewise must the deacons be grave, not doubletongued, not given to much wine, not greedy of filthy lucre; Holding the mystery of the faith in a pure conscience. And let these also first be proved; then let them use the office of a deacon, being found blameless. Even so must their wives be grave, not slanderers, sober, faithful in all things. Let the deacons be the husbands of one wife, ruling their children and their own houses well. For they that have used the office of a deacon well purchase to themselves a good degree, and great boldness in the faith which is in Christ Jesus."*

The blessing and encouragement that supportive deacons have been in the cause of Christ is priceless. The ongoing progress of many local churches is certainly due in part, if not a large part, to faithful deacons. The deacon has the wonderful privilege of being a helper to his pastor. Serving under the pastor will bring enrichment in this life and rewards in the future life.

What a blessing for any church to have spiritual pastors and spiritual and supportive deacons. They are God's team to bring blessing to any local church.

SOUL WINNING MEMBERS

Stephen and Philip are mentioned in Acts 6:5. As we study on in the book of Acts we learn that these two men were dynamic, aggressive, powerful, witnesses for the Lord. They represent the aggressive soul-winning zeal of the members of the New Testament Church. Soul-winning members characterized the early church. (More in the following chapter about **every member evangelism.**)

9

New Testament Church Members Were Soul Winners

(every member evangelism)

"For I am not ashamed of the gospel of Christ . . ."
(Romans 1:16)

". . . and at that time there was great persecution against the church which was at Jerusalem; and they were all scattered abroad . . . except the apostles . . . Therefore they that were scattered abroad went every where preaching the word."
(Acts 8:1, 4)

"For from you sounded out the word of the Lord . . ."
(I Thessalonians 1:8)

While visiting a church during a Midweek Service, the congregation was discussing the matter of witnessing. The pastor presented a basic message concerning the need for God's people to be witnesses for Christ according to the clear teaching of the Bible. During the discussion time, one of the deacons in the church said, "I don't think everyone of us is responsible to witness; I believe it is only the pastor's job and maybe a few others who have some special ability to witness; it is not everyone's job." I am sure you have heard someone express similar thoughts and attitudes about witnessing for Christ. It is the pastor's job and maybe a few others' responsibility, but certainly not mine!

Are great numbers of believers exempt from this area of service? Certainly many believers do not really think they should witness. This is evidenced by scores and scores of believers, who are members of fundamental, Bible-believing, evangelistic churches, who never seek to witness for Christ, and multitudes of believers who have never led a soul to Christ. Great numbers of these unevangelistic people are members of "evangelistic" churches.

No One Is Excluded

What does the Bible have to say about this vital matter? The Bible does **not** teach that witnessing for Christ is a gift that is possessed by only a few choice people. The Bible never teaches that only those who have the gift to witness are to witness. Witnessing is not a gift; it is a command (Matthew 28:19, 20; Mark 16:15; II Cor. 5:20). Anyone who indicates that only a select few are to witness is simply not acquainted with the plain teaching of God's Word. No one can show or prove from the Bible that only a few have the responsibility to witness. At best, it is a shallow excuse to hide behind. As someone has said: "Let's stop clutching our weaknesses, shyness, lack of training, fear, or any other excuse and start believing the God of the impossible who specializes in using weak vessels. There is not a single Christian who cannot become an effective revolutionary witness for Jesus Christ if he really wants to."[1] God in His wisdom did not excuse the majority of His children from the most urgent task in all the world.

46

In John 4, we read about the familiar *"woman at the well."* John 3 tells us about an "up and outer;" John 4 tells us about a "down and outer." It doesn't make any difference whether a person is an "up and outer" or a "down and outer," they both need to be saved. Christ stands ready to save "up and outers," as well as, "down and outers."

The woman in John 4 became an effective soul winner on the same day of her conversion. She never went to Bible school, nor did she ever have a course in personal evangelism. She may not have had the best personality, and certainly she did not have the best of parental training! However, she was a soul winner. In John 4:39 we read, *"and many of the Samaritans of that city believed on Him for the saying of the woman, which testified, He told me all that ever I did."* Not some, but many believed on Christ because of this woman. John 4 is a good chapter to study in the light of personal evangelism.

In the book of I Thessalonians, we learn about a great church, *"the church of Thessalonica."* One of the most commendable things about this exemplary church is found in I Thess. 1:7, 8, *"So that ye were ensamples to all that believe in Macedonia* (northern Greece) *and Achaia* (southern Greece). *For from you sounded out the word of the Lord not only in Macedonia and Achaia, but also in every place your faith to God-ward is spread abroad . . ."*

When people thought of this church something immediately came to mind. The thing that came to mind was **not** their outstanding pastor, great musical program, varied activities, beautiful facilities, professional staff, political involvement, etc. **They were known for their**

aggressiveness and diligence in *"sounding out the word of the Lord."* They were not only known in their immediate community but also far and wide for their persistent witnessing.

The word *"you"* in I Thess. 1:8 refers to the entire church. This church, as a unit, as a congregation, was widely known as a soul-winning local church. The emphasis is not on a few people in the church **but the church as a whole had this reputation!** How many churches have this same reputation today? The shameful thing is that many churches have reputations for various things, but very few churches have the reputation that the church of the Thessalonians had.

The Bible truth we learn from this passage is **every member evangelism.** It is God's plan for every believer to be involved in the work of evangelism. Every believer has the responsibility and obligation to be a witness for Christ. It is **every believer's** responsibility to aggressively and diligently seek to lead people to Christ. II Cor. 5:20 *"Now then we are ambassadors for Christ."*

THE PLIGHT OF THE CHURCH
SO SLOW IN LEARNING . . .

Years ago Dr. R. A. Torrey, the well-known evangelist and successor of D. L. Moody, was preaching about the need for every person in Christ, to reach those who are out of Christ. That night, after preaching about the responsibility of every believer to be an active witness for Christ, a woman came to Dr. Torrey and said excitedly, "Dr. Torrey, you are wrong; you are dead wrong! Until tonight you were my favorite preacher, but no more."

Dr. Torrey sought to calm the woman down. He said, "Why are you so upset over the message tonight?"

She said, "You said every Christian ought to be an active witness for Christ. I thoroughly disagree with that!"

Dr. Torrey asked, "Why?"

This woman, who had been a Christian for several years said, "I am a widow with three young boys. I spend all day and part of the night slaving behind my sewing machine seeking to eke out a living for me and my boys. I hardly ever leave my apartment. Dr. Torrey, how do you expect me to be a witness and soul winner when I have to spend most of my life behind a sewing machine. I have no time for visitation, etc."

Dr. Torrey asked, "Did you ever witness to the milkman or iceman?"

The woman bowed her head in shame. The Lord convicted her; she asked Dr. Torrey's forgiveness for the way she acted, and prayed and set out by God's grace to be an active witness for Christ. She realized that even though she spent most of her time behind a sewing machine she still could be a witness for Christ.

The next day her iceman, George, came to the door bright and early. She had on her best dress, the best table cloth on the table, and a large open Bible on the table with a bouquet of beautiful flowers. (She did all this so that George would ask some questions in order that she could talk to him about the Lord.) As George was leaving, he said, "I've never seen that open Bible before, and the place looks so nice."

The woman said nothing as George left. She realized she had failed to witness to George as she had set out to do. She ran to the door and called, "George! George!" He came back to the apartment. She said, "Sit down, please. George, I have known you for several years and you have been in this home many times delivering the ice, yet I have never spoken to you about your soul. George, if you died today where would you spend eternity?"

George, with tears in his eyes, said, "I have just come out of a two week revival meeting and although I knew I should have gone forward, I didn't have enough courage. I was just hoping that someone would somehow take the Bible and show me how to be saved today."

That day the widow woman, although a Christian for many years, led her very first soul to Christ, Many of us are like this woman. Although saved for many years, we are so slow in catching the soul winning vision.

So Long In Coming . . .

There was a certain home in which lived a father, a mother and five children. The youngest child was a little fair-haired, fair-skinned English boy, just barely past four years of age. The little English village in which they lived was suddenly stricken by a plague. The father in the family died first. A child died, then a second, then a third, then the fourth child. The little boy climbed up into his mother's lap.

"Mama, where is Daddy?"

"Daddy is gone. Someday we shall see him."

"Well, where is Danny?"

"Danny is gone."

"Where is Mary?"

"Mary is gone, too, to be with Daddy."

He asked where the fourth one was, only to be told, "She is gone, too, to be with Daddy."

"Mama, you aren't going to go, are you?"

She hugged him to her breast and looking down into his troubled blue eyes, she said, "Son, I may have to go."

"Mama, I will be left all alone, you can't go?"

"Son, I may have to go."

"Mama, if you go, who is going to take care of me?"

The mother, with her tears dropping on his head, sobbed out, "Jesus will take care of you, son. Jesus will take care of you, baby."

A few days later the mother was stricken and died. She was buried. No one took note of the child. Everybody was busy. The child went to sleep. Later he woke up. It was about eight or nine o'clock at night. Mama was not there, he was cold and hungry. He got out of his little bed – he still had on his clothes, of course – and went from room to room crying, "Mama! Mama!" Then he remembered where they had put his mama. He could not quite understand why. Opening the door, walking down the moonlit street, he came to the cemetery. There were no gates to bar him. Going over to his mother's fresh grave, standing by it, the lad sobbed, "Mama! Mama!"

The next morning a neighboring farmer was driving through to the next town. He dared not stop because of the pestilential air. There seemed to him too much chance of contagion, of infection. As he drove the heavily loaded wagon rather slowly, he noticed something that looked like a little animal on one of the graves by the side of the fence in the cemetery. Slowing up his horses, he saw the child. After all he was human. He had a heart. He had feelings. He jumped from the wagon, walked into the cemetery, and picked up the boy. The lad opened his eyes, saw the face of a stranger in that blue morning, and began to cry. The man petted him quiet.

"What are you doing here, son?" asked the farmer.

"I came to find Mama."

"Where is she?"

"She's in there. They put her in there. I want my Mama."

Again the great heavy tears came as the boy wept out, "Mama said that if she went away, Jesus would come and take care of me."

Pressing the child to his breast, the country man whispered as he struggled to keep the tears back, "Son, I have come to take care of you. Jesus sent me to take care of you."

Looking up through tear dimmed eyes, the boy said, "Mister, you have been a long time coming."

Spiritually speaking: could it be that we have been a long time in coming to those who are in desperate need of Christ?

TOO MANY BREAKS IN THE LINE . . .

Because we are so slow in catching the soul-winning vision, and so long in going to those in desperate need of the gospel, there are too many breaks in the line.

One summer some years ago a threshing crew of more than a hundred men, their wives and children all started out to harvest in a vast Dakota wheat field. Day after day, from sunup to sundown, they reaped the harvest of fruit that the earth yielded to them. A week went by, and a second week. Then about four o'clock one afternoon in the third week there arose a cry from the camp. "A boy is lost!" A four-year-old son of one of the couples was lost.

They asked, "Where did he go?"

The children said, "Well, we were playing hide-and-go-seek." We didn't let him play with us because he was too little. He doesn't understand. He comes back at the wrong time. He spoils our play. So we just left him alone. But he would run and hide with us. He ran with some of us. We went around and came back to the goal, but he did not come back. We didn't miss him. We kept on playing. A little while ago we missed him and went to look for him, but we couldn't find him."

The workmen knocked off from work. They unharnessed their teams. They stopped their engines, and with heavy feet and tired bodies, already fatigued with the days labor, started with the women and older children into that harvest field to find the boy. Hour after hour they tramped that grain down under their heavy feet as they kept on searching for the boy, calling to each other to see if they had found him. They went out. They came back, had a little sleep and started out again by moonlight and lantern light. All the rest of that night, and the next day, and far into the next night, and still the next morning, and that afternoon they kept on. On the third afternoon they came back worn out, so exhausted that they reeled as they walked. They said to the mother, "We have done our best. We cannot find him. Somebody must have picked him up. We will find him in a village or somebody will bring him to us. We must go back to work."

Then there stepped out from the ranks of those men a younger man. He said, "Men, I'm not trying to be smart. I know we are tired but there is one thing I just thought of that we have not tried."

They said, "What is it; what have we not tried?", smiling at him in their impatience.

He said, "Men , it is too late to work anyway. It is three o'clock. We are tired. We must get some sleep. The grain will keep. The wheat will keep. The horses and trucks will keep. Let's form a line and watch each other, not to get too far apart, and just walk into that grain field and finish out the day. When the sun goes down and we cannot see we will come back and sleep tonight and tomorrow go to work."

Well, there was not anything else they could do; there was not anything else they could think about. So they stood for a minute, raised their arms and stretched them out until their finger tips touched, spread out a little further and started into that wheat field again. They went in search until four o'clock, five o'clock, six o'clock, seven o'clock. The sun began to sink. Then came the cry, "Here he is! Here he is!" at one end of the line. They all forgot about their fatigue, their exhaustion, their tired feet, and ran to where the man was crying. And there at his feet in a little crevice overgrown by that grain was the boy, dead. They picked him up. They brought him back to the camp. They deposited him in his mother's arms. They said, "Mother, we did our best. We did our best. We don't know what else we could have done. We did our best!"

Raising her child up to God, the mother, with streaming eyes, dishevelled hair, torn-with-agony features, said,

"I am not blaming you, I've seen you do your best; but in God's name, why didn't someone think of that line before?"

The plight of the church is that too many of God's children have not taken their place in the soul-winning line that Jesus instituted over 1900 years ago and the sad result is that there are so many breaks in the line that poor lost sinners are wandering through and sinking into Hell.

EVERY MEMBER EVANGELISM

I had walked life's way with an easy tread,
Had followed where comforts and pleasures led,
Until one day in a quiet place,
I met the Master face to face.

With station and rank and wealth for my goal;
Much thought for my body but none for my soul,
I had entered to win in life's mad race,
When I met the Master face to face.

I met Him and knew Him and blushed to see,
That His eyes full of sorrow were fixed on me,
And I faltered and fell at His feet that day,
While my castles melted and vanished away.

Melted and vanished, and in their place,
Naught else did I see but the Master's face;
And I cried aloud, 'Oh, make me meet,
To follow the steps of Thy wounded feet.'

My thought is now for the souls of men;
I have lost my life to find it again,
E'er since one day in a quiet place,
I met the Master face to face.

While conducting a meeting in Florida, it was my privilege to meet and fellowship with some fine Christian people. One was a young man who had taken his place in the line of personal evangelism. The pastor mentioned that as a result of a noontime Bible Study conducted by this young man at his place of employment, he was used of God to reach several people for Christ who are now active and faithful members of his church. They were reached because a young man realized his responsibility to reach others for Christ; he took this responsibility seriously. We might say that he caught the vision of **every member evangelism.**

A great personal witness for Christ was an emigrant named Millie who lived in New York City. She was a woman of very limited talent and treasures. She scrubbed floors for a living and could hardly speak the English language.

After hearing some rousing missionary messages at her church, she went to her pastor and said, "I am ready to take the Gospel to the uttermost part of the earth. I am ready to go anywhere for my precious Saviour. Pastor, just tell me where."

The pastor did not know what to say. Surely the Lord did not want, of all people, Millie to go as a missionary. He told her to go home and really pray about the matter. He did not know what else he could say to her.

The next day Millie returned to the pastor's office. "Pastor, the Lord has answered my prayer about being a missionary. The Lord wants me to be a missionary right here in my own back yard. You see, the man who operates the restaurant is from Greece, the people who run the cleaners are from China, the people who own the dime store are Jewish, the woman who works in the grocery store is from Italy, the man who works at the hotel is from Poland. Pastor, the Lord wants me to be a missionary right here in my own neighborhood."

As Millie would go to the restaurant and get her bowl of soup and hard roll (she never had money for anything else on the menu), she would always leave a gospel tract and tell the people at the restaurant what a wonderful Saviour she had, and she never failed to let them know they would always receive a warm welcome at her church. She witnessed faithfully and persistently from place to place.

As the years passed, Millie finally went home to be with her precious Lord and Master.

The funeral arrangements were made. Some wondered if anyone would attend the funeral. The funeral took place at her church. The building was filled to overflowing. After the funeral message, just before the service was to conclude, an outstanding businessman in the community asked if he could say something. He said simply, "It was because of Millie that I am a Christian today. It was through her witness that I was saved." Several other business people and others subsequently stood and gave testimony that they were saved because of Millie's sincere, faithful, persistent, loving witness.

Millie caught the vision of **every member evangelism.**

When I enter that beautiful city,
Far removed from earth's sorrow and fear;
I want to hear somebody saying:
It was **YOU** who invited me here.

When to welcome me over the River,
The loved ones of earth should draw near,
I want to hear somebody whisper,
It was **YOU** who invited me here.

When the glad harps of heaven are ringing,
With music so tender and clear,
I want to have somebody singing;
It was **YOU** who invited me here.

To this happy home I might not have come,
Had **YOU** not invited me here.

10

New Testament Church Members Were Missionary Minded

(go into all the world and preach the gospel to every creature)

"And that repentance and remission of sins should be preached in his name among all nations . . ."
(Luke 24:4)

"The church was not designed to be a reservoir, ever receiving and retaining for itself God's spiritual blessings, but rather a conduit conveying them on and out to others everywhere. Its true mission was and must ever continue to be, the same as its Lord's to seek and save the lost, wherever these are to be found, whether at home or in distant lands."

– Robert Hall Glover

GOD'S PROGRAM OF MISSIONS IS CLEARLY DEFINED

God's program for missions is clearly defined in the Scriptures: Matthew 28:19-20 – *"Go ye therefore, and teach **all nations**, baptizing them in the name of the Father, and of the Son, and of the Holy Ghost: Teaching them to observe all things whatsoever I have commanded you: and, lo I am with you always, even unto the end of the world."* Mark 16:15 – *"And he said unto them, go ye into all the **world** and preach the Gospel to **every creature**."* Luke 24:47 – *"And that repentance* *and remission of sins should be preached in his name among **all nations** . . ."* John 20:21 – ". . . As my Father hath sent me, even so send I you." Acts 1:8 – *"But ye shall receive power, after that the Holy Ghost is come upon you: and ye shall be witnesses unto me both in Jerusalem, and in all Judea, and in Samaria, and unto the **uttermost part of the earth**."* Nothing more needs to be said.

THIS PROGRAM WAS CARRIED OUT
BY THE NEW TESTAMENT CHURCH

It is most informative to study the book of Acts from a geographical standpoint. Specifically the gospel went from Jerusalem to such interesting places as: Samaria, Gaza, Azotus, Caesarea, Damascus, Tarsus, Joppa, Lydda, Antioch, Salamis, Paphos, Cyprus, Perga, Antioch (Galatia), Iconium, Lystra, Derbe, Seleucia, Attalia, Troas, Philippi, Thessaloncia, Berea, Athens, Corinth, Cenchreae, Ephesus, Rhodes, Patara, Miletus, Assos, Ptolemais, Tyre, Sidon, Myra, Lases, Melita, Syracuse, Rhegium, Puteoli, Appii Forum, Three Taverns, Rome, Colossae, and Crete.

Just from our study of the New Testament Church, we learn that the Gospel was preached and churches were established in such modern day countries as: Israel, Syria, Turkey, Greece, Albania, Yugoslavia, Macedonia, Bulgaria, Italy, most of the modern day Mediterranean countries, and many others would be the countries evangelized by the early church. In Romans 15:24, 28, Paul talks about going to Spain.

Fundamentally, the Gospel was preached and churches established in much of the world by the early church. Paul notes the astonishing and astounding extent of Gospel outreach by the early church in Colossians 1:6, *"Which is come unto you, **as it is in all the world** . . ."* This amazing feat was accomplished without any Christian organizations or parachurch groups! Clearly, there is something here that we can learn from the New Testament Church.

Unquestionably, the New Testament Church was a missionary minded church.

GOD WANTS ALL OF OUR CHURCHES
TO BE MISSIONARY MINDED CHURCHES

Christ's command remains the same! Christ's command is our commission! Christ's command requires obedience! As the renowned Hudson Taylor once said: "The Great Commission is not an option to be considered, but rather it's a command to be obeyed."

Involvement in getting the Gospel out and establishing churches at home and abroad is God's will for all believers and all churches.

> We've a Saviour to show to the nations,
> Who the path of sorrow hath trod,
> That all of the world's great peoples,
> Might come to the truth of God!
> H. Ernest Nichol

In closing, why every Christian should be missionary minded: **1.** Man's need is the same in all the world: Romans 3:9 – *"What then? are we better than they? No, in no wise: for we have before proved both Jews and Gentiles, that they are all under sin."* Romans 3:23 – *"For all have sinned . . ."* **2.** God loves the whole world: John 3:16 – *"God so loved the world . . ."* **3.** Christ died for the whole world: I John 2:2 – *"propitiation . . . sins of the whole world."* John 1:29 – *". . . taketh* *away the sin of the world."* **4.** Salvation is offered to the whole world: John 3:16 – *". . . whosoever . . ."* Romans 10:13 – *". . . whosoever . . ."* **5.** God wills that the whole world be saved: I Timothy 2:3 – *"God . . . who will have all men to be saved."* II Peter 3:9 – *"The Lord is . . . not willing that any . . . perish."* **6.** God has told us to preach to all the world: Matthew 28:19 – *". . . all nations . . ."* Acts 1:8 – *". . . the uttermost part of the earth."* II Corinthians 10:16 – *"to preach the gospel in the regions beyond . . ."* **7.** Churches are to be established in all the world: Colossians 3:11 – *". . . neither Greek nor Jew, circumcision nor uncircumcision. Barbarian, Scythian, bond nor free . . ."* Revelation 5:9 – *"hast redeemed us to God by thy blood out of every kindred, and tongue, and people, and nation."*

11

New Testament Church Members Were Persecuted

(being a Christian is dangerous!)

"Remember the word that I said unto you, The servant is not greater than his lord. If they have persecuted me, they will also persecute you . . ."
(John 15:20)

"Think not that I am come to send peace on earth: I came not to send peace, but a sword. For I am come to set a man at variance against his father, and the daughter against her mother, and the daughter in law against her mother in law. And a man's foes shall be they of his own household."
(Matthew 10:34-36)

SOMETHING HIS FOLLOWERS COULD NOT AVOID

John 15:18 – *"If the world hate you, ye know that it hated me before it hated you."*

John 16:1, 2 – *"These things have I spoken unto you, that ye should not be offended. They shall put you out of the synagogues: yea, the time cometh, that whosoever killeth you will think that he doeth God service."*

John 17:14 – *"I have given them thy word; and the world hath hated them, because they are not of the world, even as I am not of the world."*

John 16:33 – *". . . in the world ye shall have tribulation . . ."*

No one can misunderstand these plain statements from the lips of the Master.

We Certainly Read About Persecution In The Book Of Acts

Acts 4:2, 3 – *"Being grieved that they taught the people, and preached through Jesus the resurrection from the dead. And they laid hands on them, and put them in hold unto the next day: for it was now eventide."*

Acts 4:18-21 – *"And they called them, and commanded them not to speak at all nor teach in the name of Jesus. But Peter and John answered and said unto them, Whether it be right in the sight of God to hearken unto you more than unto God, judge ye. For we cannot but speak the things which we have seen and heard. So when they had further threatened them, they let them go, finding nothing how they might punish them, because of the people: for all men glorified God for that which was done."*

Acts 5:17-18 – *"Then the high priest rose up, and all they that were with him, (which is the sect of the Sadducees) and were filled with indignation, and laid their hands on the apostles, and put them in the common prison."*

Acts 5:27-29 – *"And when they had brought them, they set them before the council: and the high priest* asked them, Saying, Did not we straitly command you that ye should not teach in this name? and, behold, ye have filled Jerusalem with your doctrine, and intend to bring this man's blood upon us. Then Peter and the other apostles answered and said, We ought to obey God rather than men."

Acts 5:40-42 – "And to him they agreed and when they had called the apostles, and beaten them, they commanded that they should not speak in the name of Jesus, and let them go. And they departed from the presence of the council, rejoicing that they were counted worthy to suffer shame for his name. And daily in the temple, and in every house, they ceased not to teach and preach Jesus Christ."

Acts 6:9 – "Then there arose certain of the synagogue, which is called the synagogue of the Libertines, and Cyrenians, and Alexandrians, and of them of Cilicia and of Asia, disputing with Stephen."

Acts 7:54, 57-59 – "When they hear these things, they were cut to the heart, and they gnashed on him with their teeth . . . Then they cried out with a loud voice, and stopped their ears, and ran upon him with one accord, and cast him out of the city, and stoned him: and the witnesses laid down their clothes at the young man's feet, whose name was Saul. And they stoned Stephen, calling upon God, and saying, Lord Jesus, receive my spirit."

Acts 8:1-3 – "And Saul was consenting unto his death. And at that time there was a great persecution against the church which was at Jerusalem; and they were all scattered abroad throughout the regions of Judea and Samaria, except the apostles. And devout men carried Stephen to his burial, and made great lamentation over him. As for Saul, he made havoc of the *church, entering into every house, and haling men and women committed them to prison."*

Acts 9:1, 2 – *"And Saul, yet breathing out threatenings and slaughter against the disciples of the Lord, went unto the high priest, And desired of him letters to Damascus to the synagogues, that if he found any of this way, whether they were men or women, he might bring them bound unto Jerusalem."*

Acts 9:16, 21 – *"For I will show him how great things he must suffer for my name's sake . . . But all that heard him were amazed, and said; Is not this he that destroyed them which called on this name in Jerusalem . . ."*

Acts 9:23-25 – *"And after that many days were fulfilled, the Jews took counsel to kill him: but their laying await was known of Saul. And they watched the gates day and night to kill him. Then the disciples took him by night, and let him down by the wall in a basket."*

Acts 11:19 – *"Now they which were scattered abroad upon the persecution that arose about Stephen . . ."*

Acts 12:1-5 – *"Now about the time Herod the king stretched forth his hands to vex certain of the church. And he killed James the brother of John with the sword. And because he saw it pleased the Jews, he proceeded further to take Peter also. (Then were the days of unleavened bread.) And when he had apprehended him, he put him in prison, and delivered him to four quaternions of soldiers to keep him . . . Peter therefore was kept in prison: but prayer was made without ceasing of the church unto God for him."*

Acts 13:10 – *". . . thou enemy of all righteousness . . ."*

Acts 13:45 – *". . . they were filled with envy, and spake against those things which were spoken by Paul, contradicting and blaspheming."*

Acts 13:50 – *"But the Jews stirred up the devout and honorable women, and the chief men of the city, and raised persecution against Paul and Barnabas, and expelled them out of their coasts."*

Acts 14:2 – *"But the unbelieving Jews stirred up the Gentiles, and made their minds evil affected against the brethren."*

Acts 14:5, 6 – *"And when there was an assault made both of the Gentiles, and also of the Jews with their rulers, to use them despitefully, and to stone them, They were aware of it, and fled unto Lystra and Derbe . . ."*

Acts 14:19 – *"And there came thither certain Jews from Antioch and Iconium, who persuaded the people, and having stoned Paul, drew him out of the city, supposing he had been dead."*

Acts 14:22 – *"Confirming the souls of the disciples, and exhorting them to continue in the faith, and that we must through much tribulation enter into the kingdom of God."*

Acts 16:2-24 – *"These men . . . exceedingly trouble our city . . . And the multitude rose up together against them: and the magistrates rent off their clothes and commanded to beat them. And when they had laid many stripes upon them, they cast them into prison charging the jailer to keep them safely . . . thrust them into the inner prison and made their feet fast in the stocks."*

Acts 16:33 – *"And he took them the same hour of*

the night, and washed their stripes; and was baptized, he and all his, straightway."

Acts 17:5 – *"But the Jews which believed not, moved with envy, took unto them certain lewd fellows of the baser sort, and gathered a company, and set all the city in an uproar, and assaulted the house of Jason, and sought to bring them out to the people."*

Acts 17:32 – *"And when they heard of the resurrection of the dead, some mocked . . ."*

Acts 18:12 – *"made insurrection with one accord against Paul, and brought him to the judgment seat . . ."*

Acts 19:24 – *"And the same time there arose no small stir about the way."*

Acts 20:1 – *"And after the uproar was ceased, Paul called unto him the disciples . . ."*

Acts 20:23 – *"Save that the Holy Ghost witnesseth in every city, saying that bonds and afflictions abide me."*

Acts 21:13 – *"Then Paul answered, What mean ye to weep and to break mine heart? for I am ready not to be bound only, but also to die at Jerusalem for the name of the Lord Jesus."*

Acts 21:30-33 – *"And all the city was moved, and the people ran together: and they took Paul . . . and as they went about to kill him . . . Then the chief captain came near, and took him, and commanded him to be bound with two chains . . ."*

Acts 21:36 – *"and the multitude of the people followed after, crying, Away with him."*

Acts 22:4 – *"And I persecuted this way unto death . . ."*

Acts 22:22, 25 – *". . . and said, Away with such a fellow from the earth: for it is not fit that he should live . . . And as they bound him with thongs, Paul said unto the centurian that stood by, Is it lawful for you to scourge a man that is a Roman, and uncondemned?"*

Acts 23:2 – *". . . commanded them that stood by him to smite him on the mouth."*

Acts 23:12-14 – *". . . and bound themselves under a curse, saying that they would neither eat nor drink till they had killed Paul . . . and there were more than forty which had made this conspiracy . . . we will eat nothing until we have slain Paul."*

Acts 24:5 – *"For we have found this man a pestilent fellow, and a mover of sedition among all the Jews throughout the world, and a ringleader of the sect of the Nazarenes."*

Acts 24:27 – *". . . left Paul bound."*

Acts 25:3 – *". . . laying wait in the way to kill him."*

Acts 25:24 – *". . . crying that he ought not to live any longer."*

Acts 26:21 – *". . . and went about to kill me."*

Acts 28:20 – *". . . because that for the hope of Israel I am bound with this chain."*

IN THE EPISTLES ALSO

Philippians 1:29 – *"For unto you it is given in the behalf of Christ, not only to believe on him, but also to suffer for his sake."*

I Thessalonians 1:6 – *". . . having received the word in much affliction . . ."*

I Thessalonians – *". . . for ye also have suffered like things of your own countrymen, even as they have of the Jews: who both killed the Lord Jesus, and their own prophets, and have persecuted us; and they please not God . . . forbidding us to speak to the Gentiles that they might be saved . . ."*

I Thessalonians 3:3, 4 – *"That no man should be moved by these afflictions: for yourselves know that we are appointed thereunto. For verily, when we were with you, we told you before that we should suffer tribulation; even as it came to pass, and ye know."*

II Thessalonians 1:4 – *". . . in all your persecutions and tribulations . . ."*

II Timothy 1:8, 12 – *". . . but be thou partaker of the afflictions of the gospel . . . for the which cause I also suffer these things: nevertheless I am not ashamed . . ."*

II Timothy 3:3 – *". . . despisers of those that are good."*

II Timothy 3:12 – *"Yea, and all that will live godly in Christ Jesus shall suffer persecution."*

Romans 8:18 – *"For I reckon that the sufferings of this present time are not worthy to be compared with the glory which shall be revealed in us."*

BEING A CHRISTIAN IS DANGEROUS!

Persecution and opposition was the norm in the New Testament Church. The Word is clear; it wasn't abnormal. Likewise, there will always be opposition in this world to anyone who Biblically seeks to live for Christ and makes an earnest effort to spread His Gospel. It is unavoidable. There is always a price to pay to be true to Christ. There was a price to pay then, and there is a price to pay today. If we are not willing to take a stand for Christ and pay the price, we simply are not following the scriptural precedent that is clearly laid down.

> Am I a soldier of the cross, a follower of
>   the Lamb?
> And shall I fear to own His cause, Or blush to
>   speak His name?
>
> Must I be carried to the skies on flowery
>   beds of ease,
> While others fought to win the prize, and
>   sailed through bloody seas?
> – Isaac Watts

It should be strongly emphasized that scriptural persecution has absolutely nothing to do with unscriptural living. It is of utmost importance to make a precise and sharp distinction between these two.

PART II
IMPORTANCE

12

The Primacy Of The Local Church

(a divine institution)

". . . my church . . ."
(Matthew 16:18)

". . . the churches of Christ . . ."
(Romans 16:16)

". . . the church of God . . ."
(I Corinthians 1:2)

". . . the church of the living God . . ."
(I Timothy 3:15)

The following brief thoughts help us gain insight into the **primacy** and **centrality** of the local church.

A DIVINE INSTITUTION

First, the local New Testament Church is a divine institution: *"the church of God which is at Corinth . . ."* (I Corinthians 1:2). The local church at Corinth was *". . . the church of God . . ."*

In Acts 18:1-11, we learn that Paul was the human instrument the Lord used to establish the church at Corinth. However, he did not view it as a human institution. To Paul it was a divine institution. We certainly learn something vital here about the indispensable significance of the local New Testament Church. It is nothing less than a divine institution. The following references are well worth pondering:

Acts 20:28 – *"Take heed therefore unto yourselves, and to all the flock, over that which the Holy Ghost hath made you overseers, to feed **the church of God**, which he hath purchased with his own blood."*

I Corinthians 11:16 – *"But if any man seem to be contentious, we have no such custom, neither **the churches of God**."*

I Corinthians 15:9 – *"for I am the least of the apostles, that am not meet to be called an apostle because I persecuted **the church of God**, and wasted it . . ."*

II Corinthians 1:1 – *"Paul, an apostle of Jesus Christ by the will of God, and Timothy our brother, unto **the church of God** which is at Corinth, with all the saints which are in all Achaia . . ."*

Galatians 1:13 – *"For ye have heard of my conversation in time past in the Jews' religion, how that beyond measure I persecuted **the church of God** and wasted it . . ."*

Although the Lord uses human instruments to begin and edify local churches, we must never fail to realize that the local New Testament church is a divine institution.

THE PILLAR AND GROUND OF THE TRUTH

Second, according to I Timothy 3:15, the local church is the pillar and ground of the truth. This verse is a strong verse for those who don't believe in the primacy of the church: *". . . the church of the living God, the pillar and ground of the truth."* That's powerful language. Paul certainly saw something in the church that many today do not see!

What was Paul telling Timothy? Obviously, Paul is talking about the local church. Previously in this same chapter he is talking about the qualifications for church leaders. He is certainly not talking about invisible pastors and deacons!

Paul looked upon the local group of believers who comprised the local church as those who were upholding the truth. The picture is one of a building: **the pillars** are responsible to hold up the structure; **the ground or support** is the foundation. The local church is the pillar and foundation of the truth.

Where is God's truth found: in philosophy, in meditation, in science, in the universities, in the various civic groups, in the many social clubs, in the political parties? Of course not! The local church is the very core, the very pillar and ground of God's truth. This is the clear teaching of I Timothy 3:15.

The local church has a crucial and significant responsibility in this world. Simply stated: the local church is the focal point of God's truth; it is the citadel of the truth; it is through the church that God promulgates and disseminates His truth. The local church is God's ordained means to propagate the truth and to preserve the truth.

Many church-related organizations and parachurch groups need to realize the truth of I Timothy 3:15. Some time ago, while looking over a follow-up manual by a well known Christian organization, I noticed that they devoted just a few of the 499 pages of this manual to the subject of the church. In those few pages, the church was covered in a very light and general manner. How sad in the light of I Timothy 3:15.

Someone who was intimately involved in a well-known Christian organization said: "Jim, we say that we are local church centered, but in reality, we are not." How many Christian organizations and parachurch groups claim to be local church centered, but in reality are only interested in promoting their own programs, personalities, and activities? (Many times at the expense and neglect of the church.)

CHRIST AND THE CHURCH INSEPARABLE

Third, Christ and the local church are inseparable. Acts 9:4 tells us that Paul heard **the voice of Christ** say, *"Saul, Saul, why persecutest thou me?"* How could Paul persecute Christ? Christ had already ascended up into heaven years earlier. Paul said in Galatians 1:13, *". . . I persecuted the church of God and wasted it."* Paul referred to the local churches as the *"churches of Christ"* (Romans 16:16). Christ and His church cannot be separated. In I Corinthians 12:27 and Colossians 1:18, 24, the church is specifically cited as the body of Christ.

GOD'S LIGHT

Fourth, according to Revelation 1:20, the church is important because it is God's light in a spiritually dark and needy world. In this passage, the seven churches of Revelation 2 and 3 are likened to seven candlesticks or lampstands. A candlestick or lampstand is the instrument to emit light. The function of the local church is to send forth God's light, to herald the Word of God, in a spiritually dark and needy world.

The local church is of paramount importance because it gives forth God's truth. Need we say more; the candlestick speaks volumes.

Fifth, Satan wants to extinguish the light! Satan wants to put the light out! According to Acts 5:3, the originator, the source, of the first internal trouble that ever took place in a local church was Satan. He loves to stir up trouble in the local church; he is an expert at it. He doesn't want the light of God's truth to dispel the darkness. It is very clear from the Scriptures that anyone seeking to cause unrest in the local church is being used of the devil whether he realizes it or not. It is interesting to note in Acts 5, that the devil did not use unbelievers, but believers, to cause trouble. The devil likes to fill hearts that cause disunity, difficulty, and unrest in local churches. (How we need to be filled with the Holy Spirit. The same word that is used in Acts 5:3 is also used in Ephesians 5:18!)

SATAN TARGETS THAT WHICH IS IMPORTANT TO GOD!

GOD'S GREAT CONCERN

Sixth, according to Revelation 2 and 3, **local churches** (not Christian organizations) **are God's great concern**. How many books have been written about everything in the book of the Revelation except the contextual truth of Chapters 2 and 3. A great deal of the book of the Revelation deals with the **primacy** and **centrality** of the New Testament Church.

The entire second and third chapters of the Revelation deal with seven actual specific local churches of John's day. The Holy Spirit was concerned enough to devote two entire chapters (and by no means are they the shortest chapters in the book) to His great concern. How sad to see these chapters spiritualized away by so many expositors. Here in God's Word, we have some pressing truth about the primacy and centrality of the local church.

It is interesting to note that nowhere in these seven letters to these seven actual churches does the Lord tell anyone to forsake any of these churches! Each local group of believers is exhorted to do what they can as individuals to make these churches what they ought to be. The key word is repent! Local churches need revival that comes through God's people repenting. (Keep in mind, that we are talking about Bible-believing local churches, not liberal or modernistic churches that are not true to the Bible. The principle of II Corinthians 6:14 and Revelation 18:4 applies to people in liberal or modernistic churches.)

The truth that local churches are God's great concern is obvious, clear, and unmistakable in Revelation 1:13, *"And in the midst of the seven candlesticks* (churches) *one like unto the Son of man . . ."*

The New Testament, not only, teaches the importance of the local church, but also, the primacy and centrality of the church. The fact that the local church was foremost and fundamental in the New Testament is clearly apparent.

13

The Local Church: God's Only Program For Planet Earth

(the apostles founded churches and they founded nothing else)

". . . the church of the living God, the pillar and ground of the truth"
(I Timothy 3:15)

GOD'S ONLY PROGRAM

The word church is used about 100 times in the new Testament. In the book of Acts alone, the word church or churches is used several times:

Acts 2:47 – *"Praising God, and having favour with all the people. And the Lord added to the **church** daily such as should be saved."*

Acts 5:11 – *"And great fear came upon all the **church**, and upon as many as heard these things."*

Acts 8:1, 3 – *"And Saul was consenting unto his death. And at that time there was a great persecution against the **church** which was at Jerusalem; and they were all scattered abroad throughout the regions of Judaea and Samaria, except the apostles. As for Saul, he made havoc of the **church** entering into every house, and hauling men and women committed them to prison."*

81

Acts 9:31 – *"Then had the **churches** rest throughout all Judaea and Galilee and Samaria, and were edified; and walking in fear of the Lord, and in the comfort of the Holy Ghost, were multiplied."*

Acts 11:22 – *"Then tidings of these things came unto the ears of the **church** which was in Jerusalem: and they sent forth Barnabas, that he should go as far as Antioch."*

Acts 11:26 – *"And when he had found him, he brought him unto Antioch. And it came to pass, that a whole year they assembled themselves with the **church**, and taught much people. And the disciples were called Christians first in Antioch."*

Acts 12:1 – *"Now about that time Herod the King stretched forth his hands to vex certain of the **church**."*

Acts 12:5 – *"Peter therefore was kept in prison: but prayer was made without ceasing of the **church** unto God for him."*

Acts 13:1 – *"Now there were in the **church** that was at Antioch certain prophets and teachers; as Barnabas, and Simeon that was called Niger, and Lucius of Cyrene, and Manaen, which had been brought up with Herod the tetrarch, and Saul."*

Acts 14:23 – *"And when they had ordained the elders in every **church**, and had prayed with fasting, they commanded them to the Lord, on whom they believed."*

Acts 14:27 – *"And when they were come, and had gathered the **church** together, they rehearsed all that God had done with them, and how he had opened the door of faith unto the Gentiles."*

Acts 15:3, 4 – *"And being brought on their way by the **church**, they passed through Phenice and Samaria, declaring the conversion of the Gentiles; and they caused great joy unto all the brethren. And when they were come to Jerusalem, they were received of the **church**, and of the apostles and elders, and they declared all things that God had done with them."*

Acts 15:22 – *"Then pleased it the apostles and elders, with the whole **church**, to send **chosen** men of their own company to Antioch with Paul and Barnabas; namely, Judas surnamed Barnabas, and Silas, chief men among the brethren:"*

Acts 15:41 – *"And he went through Syria and Cilicia, confirming the **churches**."*

Acts 16:5 – *"And so were the **churches** established in the faith, and increased in number daily."*

Acts 18:22 – *"And when he had landed at Caesarea, and gone up, and saluted the **church**, he went down to Antioch."*

Acts 20:17 – *"And from Miletus he sent to Ephesus, and called the elders of the **church**."*

Acts 20:28 – *"Take heed therefore unto yourselves, and to all the flock, over that which the Holy Ghost hath made you overseers, to feed the **church** of God, which he hath purchased with his own blood."*

Obviously, the church was foremost and fundamental in the book of Acts.

The church is not some after thought with God. It is not just a program, or even a good program for planet earth. To the early Christians, the local church was the divinely ordained unit on earth through which God chose to work and the only such unit! The local church was God's only unit on earth for propagating the faith and the disciples were content to work only within that context. Certainly, God has a wonderful plan and program for the family; He also has a definite program for civil government; however, **He has no other plan or program to carry on His work in this world apart from His church.**

RIVETING QUOTES

"It is noticeable in the book of Acts that no attempt was made to form an organization of any kind for carrying on the work of the Lord. **THE LOCAL CHURCH WAS GOD'S UNIT ON EARTH FOR PROPAGATING THE FAITH AND THE DISCIPLES WERE CONTENT TO WORK WITHIN THAT CONTEXT.** It was spiritual wisdom, **not primitive naivete** that saved the early Christians from setting up human organizations to carry on the work of the Lord."[1]

"THE APOSTLES FOUNDED CHURCHES, AND THEY FOUNDED NOTHING ELSE, because for the ends in view nothing else was required or could have been so suitable. In each place where they labored they formed the converts into a local assembly . . . **NO OTHER ORGANIZATION THAN THE LOCAL CHURCH APPEARS IN THE NEW TESTAMENT, NOR, DO WE FIND EVEN THE GERM OF ANYTHING FURTHER."[2]**

"I believe the kingdom of Christ on earth has suffered because individual men have failed to recognize the importance of the local church, and the fact that **THE CHURCH IS THE WORKING UNIT OF THE KINGDOM OF GOD ON EARTH AT THIS PRESENT TIME.**"[3]

CHRISTIAN ORGANIZATIONS AND PARACHURCH GROUPS OF HUMAN ORIGIN

There are several solid reasons why the church is God's program for planet earth and Christian organizations are not. **First**, parachurch groups have no Biblical authorization. Christian organizations are not scriptural. I realize this is hard for many to swallow; however, the New Testament is precise and definite: **GOD IN HIS WISDOM ORDAINED THE CHURCH TO CARRY ON HIS WORK IN THE WORLD TODAY.** The church is of divine origin, *". . . the church of God . . ."* (I Corinthians 1:2). We may argue and debate this point all we want; however, the Scripture is plain and clear. We can use all the **HUMAN WISDOM** we want to defend Christian organizations and parachurch groups; however, they just don't stand up under the light of Scripture.

Not a few Christian organizations are built upon good human wisdom, good psychological wisdom, and good conventional wisdom. Nevertheless, we must not make a mistake and equate these good ideas with the spiritual wisdom that is found in the Bible. Human, psychological, and conventional wisdom, as good as they may be, are not necessarily Biblical wisdom. According to James 3:15, not all wisdom is from above. I Corinthians 3:19 – *"For the wisdom of this world is foolishness with God . . ."* **God's wisdom never goes contrary to His Word!** The Word has much to say about the church; it says nothing about seeking to carry on His work apart from His church.

Parachurch groups were nonexistent in the New Testament. It is hard to get excited about something the Bible is silent about.

Second, Christian organizations are notorious for compromising the truth. Jesus told his disciples to teach *"all things"* He commanded them. My experience with Christian organizations is that they are often explicitly forbidden to teach certain basic truths. Sometimes they are not even permitted to take a stand on some elementary truths that are not even of a controversial nature. This is commonplace and wide spread. Not a few, never take a clear stand on the local church, baptism, the Lord's Supper, and other elementary truths that were clearly instituted by our blessed Lord Himself. The local church and baptism are clear aspects of the great commission according to Jesus in Matthew 28:19, 20. Are we to obey him or not?

According to Matthew 28:19, 20, the first thing we are to tell a new convert is to get in a sound church and be baptized. Maybe Matthew 28:19, 20, and the book of Acts are no longer in the Bible, or at least, not in the Bible of some of our parachurch friends.

Third, not a few Christian organizations are **parasitic**, because they encourage people to use their God-given gifts in an unscriptural place. According to Ephesians 4, God gives gifts to His church to be used for its edification. Keep in mind there are **thousands** of various parachurch groups. They come in all shapes, sizes, and varieties. A lot of gifted men are serving in the wrong place because they are not serving in a church-centered ministry. In fact, I have talked with some who have admitted this very thing. I have personally known some men who were very dissatisfied with their "service for the Lord" because they knew it was not nearly as local church centered as it should have been.

It is not a question of whether these mammoth organizations have wonderfully gifted personnel, exciting and interesting programs. The question is: Are they encouraging believers to use their God given gifts in an unscriptural place? (Specifically outside and apart from the local church.) Using one's God-given gift outside the context of the New Testament Church may build one's ego, but it is in blatant violation of Scripture. It just does not line up with the Word.

Fourth, in regards to finances, man-made alternatives to the local **church** certainly are **parasitic!** It takes enormous, vast, exorbitant sums of money to keep these organizations going! More than the average person realizes. **Think of all the money that is not being used in a Biblical way.** Often the organization is devoted to expensive maintaining rather than to the primary purpose for which it was even founded. The well worn saying, "If the founder knew what was now going on, he would turn over in his grave," applies to many Christian organizations!

It might be good to write and ask for a detailed financial statement from your favorite Christian organization. If you can get a **DETAILED ONE, WHICH IS HIGHLY UNLIKELY, YOU MAY BE SURPRISED AT WHAT YOU LEARN.**

How can so many in these various groups have a clear conscience when they are persistently begging for money (and many times not insignificant amounts). Often the only hope, assurance, and confidence that some give is the hope, assurance, and confidence of another urgent financial appeal! **IMAGINE THE APOSTLE PAUL DOING WHAT MANY ARE DOING TODAY?** Obviously, it is far removed from the New Testament pattern.

Many years ago, far too many than I would like to admit, I first read the subsequent quote and, I must say, it really got me thinking:

"New Testament giving is **church giving**. Paul uses the **churches as examples**, and not individual Christians. In verses 18-19 and 23-24 (II Corinthians 8) it is **the churches** that are emphasized. **Christian giving is church giving**, bringing tithes and offerings to **the local church** which is God's storehouse. This was the very same directions Paul gave them in I Corinthians 16:2. On the first day of the week (the Lord's Day), the believers (the Lord's people) were to bring their offerings (the Lord's tithes and offerings) to the church (the Lord's house). The words *'lay by him in store'* in I Corinthians 16:2, are the exact equivalent of the word *'storehouse'* in Malachi 3:10. Some Christians today say, 'I don't bring my tithes to the church. I let the Spirit tell me where to send them.' **DOES THE SPIRIT INSTRUCT US APART FROM THE BIBLE?** These Christians are making two mistakes: **1.** the tithe is the Lord's, not their own; and **2.** the Spirit tells us in the Word to bring His tithes to His storehouse. **SPIRITUAL GIVING IS BIBLE-BASED GIVING.** If a Christian does not bring his tithes and offerings to the local church, then his heart is not in the local church (Matthew 6:21). Individual giving outside the local church **may exalt men** and win recognition for them; but **LOCAL CHURCH GIVING exalts the Lord** and supports His **work**."[4]

Fifth, overlapping, duplication, jealously, and rivalry are common among many Christian organizations. Countless "insiders" know all too well that this is true.

In Closing

First, it is not always easy to serve the Lord in His church (however, it is uniquely rewarding!) There are always greener pastures of Christian service outside the church. Frequently, there is a lot more "glamor" serving outside the church in some grandiose ministry. Often it is hard and humbling, often difficult, to serve the Lord in His church. In II Corinthians 11:16-33, Paul is specifically talking about his suffering, and then in verse 28 he says *"besides those that are without, that which cometh upon me daily, **the care** of all the churches."* Church-centered ministry takes a lot out of a person. In Galatians 4:19, Paul says: *"My little children, of whom I **travail** in birth again until Christ be formed in you."* Sometimes things did not always go the way even the great apostle Paul would have liked them to go.

Second, local church ministry is **WHERE THE ACTION IS**; it is an "in the trenches" type ministry in comparison to other types of ministries that are far removed from the battle line. There is a sharp distinction between being involved in a Christian organization **outside one's home area**, and being involved in seeking to **evangelize, baptize,** and **stabilize** people in the very area where **YOU LIVE, WORK, AND SHOP.** There is a vast difference between being involved in good social issues and political matters, handing out literature, having radio and TV ministries, conducting camps and having rallies, **AND** winning people to Christ and forming them into a local assembly and then edifying them in that local church. From a scriptural standpoint, these two concepts are not even in the same ball park!

Third, God's plan is the best plan! Imagine if all the money, energy, time, personnel, etc., etc., that is being used by the hundreds, **IF NOT LITERALLY THOUSANDS,** of various Christian organizations, was used in local church ministry! I am sure the cause of Christ would have a greater impact here in America and a more extensive impact abroad. Think about it. Have we missed seeing the strategic importance of doing things God's way as it is clearly delineated in His Word? Why aren't we content to work within the context of the New Testament Church as the early Christians were? **DARE WE THINK THAT WE HAVE A BETTER PLAN TO DO GOD'S WORK THAN GOD'S CLEARLY PRESCRIBED PLAN?**

Although some prominent men suggest that the local church is obsolete and that modern times demand another program and plan, we can truly say that the **APOSTLES FOUNDED CHURCHES AND THEY FOUNDED NOTHING ELSE, AND THE LOCAL CHURCH IS STILL, TODAY, THE PILLAR AND GROUND OF THE TRUTH!** According to the Scriptures, the church is still God's means to fulfill His program and plan for this age.

PART III
OBLIGATIONS

14

New Testament Church Members Were Identified

(church membership: man made or God ordained?)

---

*"Then they that gladly received his word were baptized: and the same day there were **added unto them** about three thousand souls. And they **continued stedfastly** in the apostles' doctrine and **fellowship** . . ."*
(Acts 2:41, 42)

*"Then departed Barnabas to Tarsus, for to seek Saul: And when he had found him, he brought him unto Antioch. And it came to pass, that a whole year **they assembled themselves with the church**, and taught much people. And the disciples were called Christians first in Antioch."*
(Acts 11:25, 26)

Church membership is definitely taught in the New Testament. In I Corinthians 5:13, we discover that some people were without the church and some were within the church. In this passage, the subject is church discipline. Churches certainly do not discipline non-existent members! According to I Tim. 5:9, certain widows were on the church rolls. According to Hebrews 13:17, pastors have definite responsibilities toward actual members.

93

As we study the Word we discover the following specifics about New Testament church organization: **1. SERVICES and MEETINGS** (Acts 20:7, I Corinthians 14:23); **2. OFFICERS** (Philippians1:1); **3. ELECTIONS** (Acts 6:5, 6); **4. ROLLS** (I Timothy 5:9); **5. DISCIPLINE** over members (I Corinthians 5); **6. AUTHORITY** (Hebrews 13:17); **7. DOCTRINE** (Acts 2:41); **8. STANDARDS** of practice (I Corinthians 14:40); **9. SYSTEM OF FINANCES** (I Corinthians 16:1-3; II Corinthians 8, 9).

As we study the New Testament, other principles of church organization could also be uncovered and listed.

THE NORMAL THING

The normal thing for believers in the New Testament was to be associated and identified with a local church. Specifically referring to local churches, Revelation 2:7 says, *"He that hath an ear, let him hear what the spirit saith unto **the churches** . . ."*   It is always taken for granted in the New Testament that believers would be in a local church. That was assumed. Not belonging to and being identified with a local church was unnatural and abnormal. Do we ever learn about any converts in the book of Acts who did not become identified with a local church? Acts 2:41, 42 – *"Then they that gladly received his word were baptized: and the same day there were added unto them about three thousand souls. And they continued stedfastly in the apostles' doctrine and fellowship . . ."*

The following quotes are informative:

"But there is more than this intimated in Scriptures, on which we ground the assertion that the church of Christ is a **DIVINELY INSTITUTED SOCIETY**, there are express commands in Scripture leaving the believer **NO ALTERNATIVE IN THE MATTER**, and requires him to unite together with other believers in the outward and public professing of his own faith before the world. **He is not left at liberty to hide that faith within his own heart, and himself to remain alone and separated from his fellow-believers."**[1]

"One of the strongest arguments supporting church membership is the obvious fact that in the New Testament the churches are empowered with the responsibility of the discipline of believers (cf. I Corinthians 5:1-3). Paul's admonition to the Corinthian church to *'put away from among yourselves that wicked person,'* would have little meaning if, **1.** he had not been received by the church, **2.** was not publicly and officially identified with the church, and **3.** consequently, could be purged from the fellowship and privileges of church membership.

"Yes, you should join a church, a New Testament church. This is the natural instinct of a saved person (Acts 2:41). **The local church is the center of God's work in this age (I Timothy 3:15)**, and to it are committed the **two ordinances** of Christ and the power to exercise **discipline. It is important that parents be members of a sound church for the sake of the children whom God has given them."**[2]

"The most obvious example and principle is that God ordained the local church as the primary place where believers are to be nurtured and edified."[3]

"It is God's will for a Christian to be an active member of a Christian fellowship. This is indicated by the fact that God has given in His Word instructions for the organization and work of a local church. Furthermore, since the church is the body through which Christ works (I Corinthians 12:27) and God's representative in the world (II Corinthians 5:19, 20), it is God's will for every Christian to be a part of it."[4]

"But I do say as plainly as I know how that every Christian ought to join in with some local congregation of Born-again Christians. He ought to do this for his own good and the good of other Christians, and to help carry on the work of Jesus Christ. First, a Christian needs Christian fellowship and Christian company. Second, one needs the public services of the church. Third, the Christian needs a pastor."[5]

"But each individual Christian needs the fellowship of individual fellow believers. The outward expression of this fellowship is in membership in some organized body of believers. If we hold aloof from all organized churches, we deceive ourselves. We will miss the helpfulness that comes from intimate union with some local congregation. I have known many well-meaning persons who have held aloof from membership . . . **and I have never known a person who has done this, whose own spiritual life has not suffered.** If you have really received Jesus Christ, hunt up, as soon as possible, some company of those who have received Jesus Christ and unite yourself with them."[6]

Clearly it is God's will for every believer to be a member of a local church. *"Not forsaking the assembling of ourselves together..."* (Hebrews 10:25). Church membership is God ordained, not man made. The early believers *"assembled themselves with the church"* (Acts 11:26).

15

New Testament Church Members Were Faithful

(is unfaithfulness a sin?)

"Not forsaking the assembling of ourselves together, as the manner of some is; but exhorting one another . . ."
(Hebrews 10:25)

". . . we have done that which was our duty to do."
(Luke 17:10)

To note how far we have departed from basic Christianity, today there are many people (some well known and popular) who actually call themselves Christians and seldom attend church!

In spite of all the professing Christians who rarely attend church regularly, and all the TV addicts, and all the sports nuts, and all the Sunday: soccer, football, baseball, softball, and basketball leagues, and in spite of all the Sunday birthday parties, and Sunday family get-to-gethers, and all the Sunday retirement banquets, etc., etc., I would like to ask the question: Is it a sin if I do not faithfully attend church every time the church door is open? Is it a sin if I do not attend every Sunday morning, Sunday night, and Wednesday night, or whenever my church has its stated services? **Is it a sin?**

Yes, it is a sin!

AM I REALLY LOYAL TO CHRIST?

As we study Acts 9:4 and Galatians 1:13, it is clear that Paul demonstrated his attitude to Christ by his attitude to the church. At this present time, we demonstrate our faithfulness to Christ by our faithfulness to His church which is His body (Colossians 1:18, 24).

If I am not faithful, it is a sin because my unfaithfulness reveals that I am not loyal to Jesus Christ. **We visibly and openly demonstrate our loyalty to Jesus Christ by our faithfulness to His church.** The local church today is His church and His body (Romans 16:16; I Corinthians 12:27).

GOD'S PROGRAM FOR BELIEVERS

The Scripture is clear that God has not only instituted the church, but that He also has given gifts to the church for the edification of its members. This truth is clearly seen in Ephesians 4:11, 12. There certainly is such a gift as the gift of the pastor. The word *"pastor"* is a good Biblical word. One of the duties of the pastor is to feed the flock (Acts 20:28). When I do not faithfully attend the local church, I am sinning against the precise program that God has instituted for my spiritual development and growth.

EDIFY ONE ANOTHER

I Thessalonians 5:11 – *"edify one another."* Am I really edifying, helping, building up other believers when I do not attend church regularly? To ask the question is to answer it. We do have an obligation and responsibility to set the right example for other believers.

Romans 14:13 warns about being a stumblingblock.

ARE WE DESTROYING THE FAITH OF OUR CHILDREN?

When we are unfaithful, what message are we sending to our children? The message that the Lord Jesus Christ, the church, the things of God, the work of the Lord, are really not important comes through loud and clear! Money, hobbies, football, recreational activities, worldly entertainment, TV, etc., are more important than the things of the Lord!

No parent is fully following the clear exhortations to teach their children in the right way if they are not faithful in their church attendance (Proverbs 22:6). How can a mother and father say they are really training their children in the right way if they do not attend church faithfully?

Many times, children learn more by what they see, or don't see, than by what they are told.

> I took a piece of plastic clay,
> And idly fashioned it one day,
> And as my fingers pressed it still,
> It moved and yielded to my will.
>
> I came again when days were past –
> The bit of clay was hard at last;
> The form I gave it, it still bore,
> But, I could change that form no more.
>
> I took a piece of living clay,
> and gently formed it day by day,
> And molded with my power and art,
> A young child's soft and yielding heart.
>
> I came again when years were gone –
> It was a man I looked upon;
> He still that early impress wore,
> And I could change him nevermore.
>
> – Author Unknown

The faith of more than a few children has been destroyed and may never be retrieved because of unfaithful parents. Parents can really do a lot to hurt and harm the faith of their children and give them a totally unbiblical view of what Christianity is all about.

How sad, that some parents only choose to go to church when it's convenient, and some find the slightest excuse to stay home.

The testimony of Josef Gabor should be a challenge to everyone. Josef grew up in Czechoslovakia when it was dominated by communism, and Christianity was despised as weakness. His father taught communist doctrine classes. But Josef's mother, who believed in Jesus Christ, took Josef and his brother faithfully to church every Sunday. They got up early each Sunday morning and took a three-hour train ride to Prague. Then they walked to the church and sat through a two and a half hour service. After eating lunch in a nearby park, they returned to church for another two and a half hour meeting. Then they took the three hour ride home.

Today, Josef Gabor is a missionary to his own people in Czechoslovakia. When he tells about going to church as a child, his eyes fill with tears of gratitude for a mother who set the right example.

One of the best ways to set the right example and be a bridge builder for our children is to be faithful in our church attendance.

> An old man, going a lone highway,
> Came, at the evening, cold and grey,
> To a chasm, vast, and deep, and wide,
> Through which was flowing a sullen tide.

The old man crossed in the twilight dim;
The sullen stream had no fears for him;
But he turned, when safe on the other side,
And built a bridge to span the tide.

"Old man," said a fellow pilgrim, near,
"You are wasting strength with building here;
Your journey will end with the ending day;
You never again must pass this way;
You have crossed the chasm, deep and wide –
Why build you the bridge at eventide?"

The builder lifted his old grey head:
"Good friend, in the path I have come," he said,
"There followeth after me today,
A youth, whose feet must pass this way.

This chasm, that has been naught to me,
To that fair-haired youth may a pitfall be.
He, too, must cross in the twilight dim;
Good friend, I am building the bridge for him."
– Will Allen Dromgoole

Josef Gabor's mother was a wise bridge builder.

THE BIBLE PLAINLY SAYS IT IS A SIN

*"Not forsaking the assembling of ourselves together,
as the manner of some is; but exhorting one another;
and so much the more, as ye see the day approaching"*
(Hebrews 10:25). Encouraging people to be faithful in
church attendance is the right and proper thing to do,
because according to Hebrews 10:25, it is the scriptural
thing to do. When we are not faithful in assembling
ourselves together, we are not following the clear teaching
of the Bible. Acts 2:42 – *". . . They continued stead-
fastly in the apostles doctrine and fellowship . . ."*

103

Do we need to make a holy vow to God in this specific area? For the sake of Jesus Christ, for the sake of other believers, certainly for the sake of our children, and for our own spiritual good, we should make a holy vow to be faithful. It is something we should do immediately.

NEEDED: MODERN DAY ERIC LIDDELS!

Years ago, a boy by the name of Eric Liddel made a vow to God that he would honor the Lord on His day. As the years passed, Scotland's greatest athlete, Eric Liddell, under intensive and unreasonable pressure, brought great honor to the Lord Jesus Christ because he determined to honor the Lord on the Lord's day by refusing to run on Sunday, choosing rather to be in the house of God with the people of God. Although the 1924 Olympic Games have long since been forgotten, the courage and faithfulness of Eric Liddell still shines brightly. Oh, how we need more modern day Eric Liddells!

Someday when we stand before the Lord, how do we ever expect to hear that *"good and faithful servant"* if we haven't even been faithful in the basic matter of church attendance. The very basic meaning of the New Testament word for church is **ASSEMBLY.**[1]

16

New Testament Church Members Were Generous

(where should we do our giving?)

"For God so loved the world that he gave . . ."
(John 3:16)

*"Therefore, as ye abound in every thing . . .
see that ye abound in this grace* (the grace
of giving) *also."*
(II Corinthians 8:7)

"For ye know the grace (generosity) *of our
Lord Jesus Christ, that though he was rich,
yet for our sakes he became poor, that ye
through his poverty might be rich."*
(II Corinthians 8:9)

". . . God loveth a cheerful giver."
(II Corinthians 9:7)

*"But the natural man receiveth not the
things of the spirit of God; for they are
foolishness unto him . . ."*
(II Corinthians 2:14)

We learn in Philippians 4:18, one way we can please
God is by our giving. We either please God, or displease
Him, by our giving.

In Luke 21:1-4, when the poor widow gave her two mites, Jesus said she gave more than all the rich people together. The Lord not only evaluates our giving by what we actually give, but also, by how much we have left over after we give.

Who Is Obligated To Give?

Only those who are saved (II Corinthians 8:5).

A Word About Tithing

The clear teaching of the Old Testament is that the tithe is the Lord's and it is most Holy unto Him (Leviticus 27:30). When the people were right with God they tithed; when they were not right with God they did not tithe. Revival always brought the people back to the principle of tithing (II Chronicles 31:1, 5, 6, 12; Nehemiah 13:11, 12; Malachi 3:7-12). To study these convicting passages is to be challenged by them!

There are some who teach that because we are under grace and not under the Old Testament law, we today should not practice tithing. The thinking goes something like this: Under grace we don't have to give what was the minimum, 10%, or the tithe, as the Jewish people did.

It is important to keep in mind that tithing did not originate under the law of Moses; it was in existence hundreds of years before the law was given. Genesis 14:20 and 28:20-22, are clear that both Abraham and Jacob practiced tithing hundreds of years before the law was given to Moses. F. B. Meyer has a pointed comment concerning Abraham's tithing: "This ancient custom shames us Christians. The patriarch (Abraham) gave more to the representative of Christ (Melchizedek) than many of us give to Christ Himself. Come, if you have never done so before, resolve to give your Lord a tithe of your . . . income . . ."[1]

Jesus commended the tithe by saying *"these ought ye to have done . . ."* in Matthew 23:23.

The *"even so"* of I Corinthians 9:14, compared with Numbers 18:21, is a clear reference to tithing in the New Testament.

As we study the early church, it is obvious that the New Testament Church believed in the tithe as the **MINIMUM STANDARD OF CHRISTIAN GIVING.**

> "Most people are agreed that if we could find out the practice of the early Christian church, it would make a good pattern to follow. To that end we examined the teachings of the early church fathers, those who were thinking and leading the people and found that on the whole the most influential of them advocated **THE TITHE AS THE MINIMUM STANDARD OF GIVING.** Thus, we have found that neither in pagan or sacred history do we have even a suggestion of less than a tithe as a standard of giving to deity. If this is true, shall we who call ourselves Christians, who bear the name of Christ, who enjoy the sunshine of God's love, who have been favored above all other people; shall we give less than they? Let us see that the tithe is **minimum standard** of our giving, and then let us ask God to enable us to increase the proportion as He prospers us, until our giving becomes truly Christian, and truly an honor to Christ and His cause."[2]

The tithe as **THE MINIMUM STANDARD OF CHRISTIAN GIVING** is not only taught by some "strong local church pastors." Many who are **NOT** pastors also teach the tithe as the minimum standard of Christian giving.[3]

Beyond The Tithe: Calvary Giving

The tithe is a good place to begin and a bad place to stop! *". . . as I have given order to the churches of Galatia, even so do ye. Upon the first day of the week let every one of you lay by him in store, as God hath prospered him . . ."* (I Corinthians 16:1, 2). *"as God hath prospered him"* seems to indicate that our giving should go **BEYOND THE TITHE. THE MORE WE HAVE THE MORE WE SHOULD GIVE.**

Specifically teaching about giving, Paul in II Corinthians 8:7-9 says, *". . . see that ye abound in this grace* (giving) *also. I speak not by commandment, but by occasion of the forwardness of others, and to prove the sincerity of your love. For ye know the grace* (generosity) *of our Lord Jesus Christ, that, though he was rich, yet for your sakes he became poor, that, ye through his poverty might be rich."* These verses are clear: Christ was so generous to us that he gave all he had for our sakes that we through His poverty might be eternally rich! Here Paul is reminding us that we ought to give in the light of how Christ gave Himself for us. **GIVING IN THE LIGHT OF CALVARY SEEMS TO BE THE THRUST.** Giving as Christ gave Himself for us, the true standard of giving, the highest standard of giving, the ultimate standard, the most spiritual level of giving. Giving from the foot of the old rugged cross approaches giving from a totally different perspective: **A PERSPECTIVE FAR SUPERIOR TO SIMPLY TITHING!**

What a concept! What a challenge! Sometimes we talk about it, and frequently we sing about it.

When I survey the wondrous cross on which
the Prince of glory died,
My richest gain I count but loss, and poor
contempt on all my pride.
Were the whole realm of nature mine, that
were a present far too small;
Love so amazing, so divine, demands my
soul, my life, my all.

– Isaac Watts

When we sing that outstanding consecration hymn, "Take My Life, and Let It Be" by Frances Ridley Havergal, we frequently sing the fourth stanza:

Take my silver and my gold,
Not a mite would I withhold . . .

It is one thing to sing about giving in the light of Calvary; it is quite another thing to practice it!

In a word: we should be very generous, extremely sacrificial, and exceedingly liberal in our giving.

If this is scriptural and right, **and Christ is our example**, then radical changes in our giving practices are absolutely necessary.

WHERE SHOULD WE DO OUR GIVING?

All the giving in the New Testament was done in and through **THE CHURCH!** No question about it; New Testament giving was **CHURCH GIVING.** As we study the New Testament we learn that Paul used **CHURCHES** as examples to challenge people to give; he never used individuals as examples (I Corinthians 16:1; II Corinthians 8:1-4, 18-19, 23-24). He never appealed to an individual for a gift! He did encourage **CHURCHES** to give (I Corinthians 16:1; I Corinthians 8, 9). In Paul's mind, giving was a **CHURCH CENTERED** matter. Scriptural giving is **church giving.**

Please don't think that only some "staunch local church pastors" teach local church giving. Not a few, who are **NOT** pastors, have come to a somewhat similar, though weaker, position.[4]

New Testament giving is local church giving. **NO OTHER TYPE OF GIVING IS EVEN HINTED AT IN THE NEW TESTAMENT.**

AMERICAN LIFE STYLES AND GIVING

Statistics reveal that many Christians fall far short from the standards laid down in the Word. There are at least two reasons for this. I am sure many more should be given. First, **Ridiculous Materialism!** Ridiculous materialism is certainly a fast spreading disease in most churches. Many are infected with it and don't even know it. Not a few eagerly buy expensive new cars and commonly eat out in high priced restaurants, and proportionately give little to the Lord's work. Placing our values on temporal things rather than eternal things is not right.

> I counted dollars while
> God counted crosses.
> I counted gains while
> He counted losses.
>
> I counted my possessions by
> The things gained in store.
> But He valued me by
> The scars that I bore.
>
> I counted my honors
> And sought for ease,

He wept while He counted
The hours on my knees.

And I never knew until
One day by a grave,
How vain are these things
We spend a lifetime to save.

Another problem is **HOARDING.** Hoarding wealth-money – is sin! Jesus specifically addressed the sin of hoarding in Matthew 6:19-21 – *"Lay not up for ourselves treasures upon earth, where moth and rust doth corrupt, and where thieves break through and steal; But lay up for yourselves treasures in heaven, where neither moth nor rust doth corrupt, and thieves do not break through and steal; For where your treasure is there will your heart be also."* **IMAGINE IF GOD HAD BEEN LIKE SO MANY OF US AND HOARDED HIS WEALTH** by keeping His Son in Glory! We would have all gone to hell!

Out of this life I shall never take
Things of silver and gold I make;
ALL that I cherish and hoard away,
After I leave, on earth must stay.

Though I call it mine, and boast its worth,
I must give it up when I quit the earth,
ALL that I gather and **all** that I keep
I just leave behind when I fall asleep.

I wonder often just what I shall own
In that other life when I pass alone,
What Jesus shall find and what He shall see
In my soul that answers the call for me.

Shall the great judge learn, when I am
    through,

That my life has gathered riches too?
Or shall at the last it be mine to find,
That **all** I had worked for I left behind?

Only a spiritually minded person can understand this subject. It was hard for the disciples; they were critical of one of the greatest acts of giving in all the Bible (Matthew 26:6-13). (Please check out this passage; it is powerful!) Paul indicated that the Corinthians were not abounding in this specific area (II Corinthians 8:7). They abounded in faith, utterance, knowledge, and in all diligence, and in love; however, they did not abound in the grace of giving. It is possible to excel in many areas of the Christian life and still come up short in the area of giving. Do we excel in this matter; or, do we come up short in the grace of giving?

APPENDICES

APPENDIX A

Chronological list of every mention of the word **church** (**ekklesia**) in the New Testament (75 times)

Matthew 16:18 – *"And I say also unto thee, That thou are Peter, and upon this rock I will build my **church;** and the gates of hell shall not prevail against it."*

Matthew 18:17 – *"And if he shall neglect to hear them, tell it unto the **church**, let him be unto thee as an heathen man and a publican."*

Acts 2:47 – *"Praising God, having favor with all the people. And the Lord added to the **church** daily such as should be saved."*

Acts 5:11 – *"And great fear came upon all the **church**, and upon as many as heard these things."*

Acts 7:38 – *"This is he, that was in the **church** in the wilderness with the angel which spake to him in the mount Sinai, and with our fathers: who received the lively oracles to give unto us:"*

Acts 8:1 – *"And Saul was consenting unto his death. And at that time there was a great persecution against the **church** which was at Jerusalem; and they were all scattered abroad throughout the regions of Judaea and Samaria, except the apostles"*

Acts 8:3 – *"As for Saul, he made havoc of the **church**, entering into every house, and hailing men and women committed them to prison."*

Acts 11:22 – *"Then tidings of these things came unto the ears of the **church** which was in Jerusalem: and they sent forth Barnabas, that he should go as far as Antioch."*

Acts 11:26 – *"And when he had found him, he brought him unto Antioch. And it came to pass, that a whole year they assembled themselves with the **church**, and taught much people. And the disciples were called Christians first in Antioch."*

Acts 12:1 – *"Now about that time Herod the king stretched forth his hands to vex certain of the church."*

Acts 12:5 – *"Peter therefore was kept in prison: but prayer was made without ceasing of the church unto God for him."*

Acts 13:1 – *"Now there were in the church that was at Antioch certain prophets and teachers; as Barnabas, and Simeon that was called Niger, and Lucius of Cyrene, and Manaen, which had been brought up with Herod the tetrarch, and Saul."*

Acts 14:23 – *"And when they had ordained the elders in every church, and had prayed with fasting, they commended them to the Lord, on whom they believed."*

Acts 14:27 – *"And when they were come, and had gathered the church together, they rehearsed all that God had done with them, and how he had opened the door of faith unto the Gentiles."*

Acts 15:3 – *"And being brought on their way by the church, they passed through Phoenicia and Samaria, declaring the conversion of the Gentiles: and they caused great joy unto all the brethren."*

Acts 15:4 – *"And when they were come to Jerusalem, they were received of the church, and of the apostles and elders, and they declared all things that God had done with them."*

Acts 15:22 – *"Then pleased it the apostles and elders, with the whole church, to send chosen men of their own company to Antioch with Paul and Barnabas; namely, Judas surnamed Barnabas, and Silas, chief men among the brethren."*

Acts 18:22 – *"And when he had landed at Casarea, and gone up, and saluted the church, he went down to Antioch."*

Acts 20:17 – *"And from Miletus he sent to Ephesus, and called the elders of the church."*

Acts 20:28 – *"Take heed therefore unto yourselves, and to all the flock, over the which the Holy Ghost hath made you overseers, to feed the church of God, which he hath purchased with his own blood."*

Romans 16:1 – *"I commend unto you Phebe our sister, which is a servant of the church which is at Cenchrea:"*

Romans 16:5 – *"Likewise greet the church that is in their house. Salute my well-beloved Epaenetus, who is the firstfruits of Achaia unto Christ."*

Romans 16:23 – *"Gaius mine host, and of the whole church, saluteth you. Erastus the chamberlain of the city saluteth you, and Quartus a brother."*

I Corinthians 1:2 – *"Unto the church of God which is at Corinth, to them that are sanctified in Christ Jesus, called to be saints, with all that in every place call upon the name of Jesus Christ our Lord, both theirs and ours:"*

I Corinthians 4:17 – *"For this cause have I sent unto you Timotheus, who is my beloved son, and faithful in the Lord, who shall bring you into remembrance of my ways which be in Christ, as I teach everywhere in every church."*

I Corinthians 6:4 – *"If then ye have judgments of things pertaining to this life, set them to judge who are least esteemed in the church."*

I Corinthians 10:32 – *"Give none offense, neither to the Jews, nor to the Gentiles, nor to the church of God:"*

I Corinthians 11:18 – *"For first of all, when ye come together in the church, I hear that there be divisions among you; and I partly believe it."*

I Corinthians 11:22 – *"What? have ye not houses to eat and drink in? or despise ye the church of God, and shame them that have not? What shall I say to you? shall I praise you in this? I praise you not."*

I Corinthians 12:28 – *"And God hath set some in the church, first apostles, secondarily prophets, thirdly teachers, after that miracles, then gifts of healings, helps, governments, diversities of tongues."*

I Corinthians 14:4 – *"He that speaketh in an unknown tongue edifieth himself; but he that prophesieth edifieth the church."*

I Corinthians 14:5 – *"I would that ye all spake with tongues, but rather that ye prophesied: for greater is he that prophesieth than he that speaketh with tongues, except he interpret, that the **church** may receive edifying."*

I Corinthians 14:12 – *"Even so ye, forasmuch as ye are zealous of spiritual gifts, seek that ye may excel to the edifying of the **church**."*

I Corinthians 14:19 – *"yet in the **church** I had rather speak five words with my understanding, that by my voice I might teach others also, than ten thousand words in an unknown tongue."*

I Corinthians 14:28 – *"But if there be no interpreter, let him keep silence in the **church**; and let him speak to himself, and to God."*

I Corinthians 14:35 – *"And if they will learn anything let them ask their husbands at home: for it is a shame for women to speak in the **church**."*

I Corinthians 15:9 – *"For I am the least of the apostles, that am not meet to be called an apostle, because I persecuted the **church** of God."*

I Corinthians 16:19 – *"The churches of Asia salute you. Aquila and Priscilla salute you much in the Lord, with the **church** that is in their house."*

II Corinthians 1:1 – *"Paul, an apostle of Jesus Christ by the will of God, and Timothy our brother, unto the **church** of God which is at Corinth, with all the saints which are in all Achaia:"*

Galatians 1:13 – *"For ye have heard of my conversation in time past in the Jews' religion, how that beyond measure I persecuted the **church** of God, and wasted it:"*

Ephesians 1:22 – *"And hath put all things under his feet, and gave him to be the head over all things to the **church**,"*

Ephesians 3:10 – *"To the intent that now unto the principalities and powers in heavenly places might be known by the **church** the manifold wisdom of God,"*

Ephesians 3:21 – *"Unto him be glory in the **church** by Christ Jesus throughout all ages, world without end. Amen."*

Ephesians 5:23 – *"For the husband is the head of the wife, even as Christ is the head of the **church:** and he is the saviour of the body."*

Ephesians 5:24 – *"Therefore as the **church** is subject unto Christ, so let the wives be to their own husbands in everything."*

Ephesians 5:25 – *"Husbands love your wives, even as Christ also loved the **church**, and gave himself for it:"*

Ephesians 5:27 – *"That he might present it to himself a glorious **church**, not having spot, or wrinkle, or any such thing; but that it should be holy and without blemish."*

Ephesians 5:29 – *"For no man ever yet hated his own flesh; but nourisheth and cherisheth it, even as the Lord the **church:**"*

Ephesians 5:32 – *"This is a great mystery: but I speak concerning Christ and the **church**."*

Philippians 3:6 – *"Concerning zeal, persecuting the **church**; touching the righteousness which is in the law, blameless."*

Philippians 4:15 – *"Now ye Philippians know also, that in the beginning of the gospel, when I departed from Macedonia, no **church** communicated with me as concerning giving and receiving, but ye only."*

Colossians 1:18 – *"And he is the head of the body, the **church**: who is the beginning, the firstborn from the dead; that in all things he might have the preeminence."*

Colossians 1:24 – *"Who now rejoice in my sufferings for you, and fill up that which is behind of the afflictions of Christ in my flesh for his body's sake, which is the **church:**"*

Colossians 4:15 – *"Salute the brethren which are in Laodicea, and Nymphas, and the **church** which is in his house."*

Colossians 4:16 – *"And when this epistle is read among you, cause that it be read also in the **church** of the Laodiceans; and that ye likewise read the epistle from Laodicea."*

II Thessalonians 1:1 – *"Paul, and Silvanus, and Timotheus, unto the church of the Thessalonians in God our Father and the Lord Jesus Christ:"*

I Timothy 3:5 – *"(For if a man know not how to rule his own house, how shall he take care of the church of God?)"*

I Timothy 5:16 – *"If any man or woman that believeth have widows, let them relieve them, and let not the church be charged; that it may relieve them that are widows indeed."*

Philemon 2 – *"And to our beloved Apphia, and Archippus our fellow soldier, and to the church in thy house:"*

Hebrews 2:12 – *"Saying, I will declare thy name unto my brethren, in the midst of the church will I sing praise unto thee."*

Hebrews 12:23 – *"To the general assembly and church of the firstborn, which are written in heaven, and to God the Judge of all, and to the spirits of just men made perfect,"*

James 5:14 – *"Is any sick among you? let him call for the elders of the church; and let them pray over him, anointing him with oil in the name of the Lord:"*

I Peter 5:13 – *"The church that is at Babylon, elected together with you, saluteth you; and so doth Marcus my son."*

III John 6 – *"Which have borne witness of thy charity before the church: whom if thou bring forward on their journey after a godly sort, thou shalt do well:"*

III John 9 – *"I wrote unto the church: but Diotrephes, who loveth to have the preeminence among them, receiveth us not."*

III John 10 – *"Wherefore, if I come, I will remember his deeds which he doeth, prating against us with malicious words: and not content therewith, neither doeth he himself receive the brethren, and forbiddeth them that would, and casteth them out of the church."*

Revelation 2:1 – *"Unto the angel of the church of Ephesus write; These things saith he that holdeth the seven stars in his right hand, who walketh in the midst of the seven golden candlesticks:"*

Revelation 2:8 – *"And unto the angel of the* **church** *in Smyrna write; These things saith the first and the last, which was dead, and is alive;"*

Revelation 2:12 – *"And to the angel of the* **church** *in Pergamos write; These things saith he which hath the sharp sword with two edges;"*

Revelation 2:18 – *"And unto the angel of the* **church** *in Thyatira write; These things saith the Son of God, who hath his eyes like unto a flame of fire, and his feet like fine brass;"*

Revelation 3:1 – *"And unto the angel of the* **church** *in Sardis write; These things saith he that hath the seven Spirits of God, and the seven stars; I know thy works, that thou hast a name, that thou livest, and art dead."*

Revelation 3:7 – *"And to the angel of the* **church** *in Philadelphia write; These things saith he that is holy, he that is true, he that hath the key of David, he that openeth, and no man shutteth; and shutteth, and no man openeth;"*

Revelation 3:14 – *"And unto the angel of the* **church** *of the Laodiceans write; These things saith the Amen, the faithful and true witness, the beginning of the creation of God;"*

APPENDIX B

Chronological list of every mention of the word **churches (ekklesias)** in the New Testament (37 times)

Acts 9:31 – *"Then had the **churches** rest throughout all Judaea and Galilee and Samaria, and were edified; and walking in the fear of the Lord, and in the comfort of the Holy Ghost, were multiplied."*

Acts 15:41 – *"And he went through Syria and Cilicia, confirming the **churches**."*

Acts 16:5 – *"And so were the **churches** established in the faith, and increased in number daily."*

Acts 19:37 – *"For ye have brought hither these men, which are neither robbers of **churches**, nor yet blasphemers of your goddess."*

Romans 16:4 – *"Who have for my life laid down their own necks: unto whom not only I give thanks, but also all the **churches** of the Gentiles."*

Romans 16:16 – *"Salute one another with an holy kiss. The **churches** of Christ salute you."*

I Corinthians 7:17 – *"But as God hath distributed to every man, as the Lord hath called everyone, so let him walk. And so ordain I in all **churches**."*

I Corinthians 11:16 – *"But if any man seem to be contentious, we have no such custom, neither the **churches** of God."*

I Corinthians 14:33 – *"For God is not the author of confusion, but of peace, as in all **churches** of the saints."*

I Corinthians 14:34 – *"Let your women keep silence in the **churches**: for it is not permitted unto them to speak; but they are commanded to be under obedience, as also saith the law."*

I Corinthians 16:1 – *"Now concerning the collection for the saints, as I have given order to the **churches** of Galatia, even so do ye."*

I Corinthians 16:19 – *"The **churches** of Asia salute you. Aquila and Priscilla salute you much in the Lord, with the church that is in their house."*

II Corinthians 8:1 – *"Moreover, brethren, we do you wit of the grace of God bestowed on the **churches** of Macedonia;"*

II Corinthians 8:18 – *"And we have sent with him the brother, whose praise is in the Gospel throughout all the **churches**;"*

II Corinthians 8:19 – *"And not that only, but who was also chosen of the **churches** to travel with us with this grace, which is administered by us to the glory of the same Lord, and declaration of your ready mind:"*

II Corinthians 8:23 – *"Whether any do inquire of Titus, he is my partner and fellow helper concerning you: or our brethren be inquired of, they are the messenger of the **churches**, and the glory of Christ."*

II Corinthians 8:24 – *"Wherefore show ye to them, and before the **churches**, the proof of your love, and of our boasting on your behalf."*

II Corinthians 11:8 – *"I have robbed other **churches**, taking wages of them, to do you service."*

II Corinthians 11:28 – *"Beside those things that are without, that which cometh upon me daily, the care of all the **churches** ."*

II Corinthians 12:13 – *"For what is it wherein ye were inferior to other **churches**, except it be that I myself was not burdensome to you? forgive me this wrong."*

Galatians 1:2 – *"And to all the brethren which are with me, unto the **churches** of Galatia:"*

Galatians 1:22 – *"And was unknown by face unto the **churches** of Judea which were in Christ:"*

I Thessalonians 2:14 – *"For ye, brethren, became followers of the **churches** of God which in Judea are in Christ Jesus: for ye also have suffered like things of your own countrymen, even as they have of the Jews:"*

II Thessalonians 1:4 – *"So that we ourselves glory in you in the **churches** of God for your patience and faith in all your persecutions and tribulations that ye endure:"*

Revelation 1:4 – *"John to the seven **churches** which are in Asia: Grace be unto you, and peace, from him which is, and which was, and which is to come; and from the seven Spirits which are before his throne;"*

Revelation 1:11 – *"Saying, I am Alpha and Omega, the first and the last: and, What thou seest, write in a book, and send it unto the seven **churches** which are in Asia; unto Ephesus, and unto Smyrna, and unto Pergamos, and unto Thyatira, and unto Sardis, and unto Philadelphia, and unto Laodicea."*

Revelation 1:20 – *"The mystery of the seven stars which thou sawest in my right hand, and the seven golden candlesticks. The seven stars are the angels of the seven **churches**: and the seven candlesticks which thou sawest are the seven **churches**."*

Revelation 2:7 – *"He that hath an ear, let him hear what the Spirit saith unto the **churches**: To him that overcometh will I give to eat of the tree of life, which is in the midst of the paradise of God."*

Revelation 2:11 – *"He that hath an ear, let him hear what the Spirit saith unto the **churches**: He that overcometh shall not be hurt of the second death."*

Revelation 2:17 – *"He that hath an ear, let him hear what the spirit saith unto the **churches**: To him that overcometh will I give to eat of the hidden manna, and will give him a white stone, and in the stone a new name written, which no man knoweth saving he that receiveth it."*

Revelation 2:23 – *"And I will kill her children with death; and all the **churches** shall know that I am he which searcheth the reins and hearts: and I will give unto every one of you according to your works."*

Revelation 2:29 – *"He that hath an ear, let him hear what the Spirit saith unto the **churches**."*

Revelation 3:6 – *"He that hath an ear, let him hear what the Spirit saith unto the **churches**."*

Revelation 3:13 – *"He that hath an ear, let him hear what the Spirit saith unto the **churches**."*

Revelation 3:22 – *"He that hath an ear, let him hear what the Spirit saith unto the **churches**."*

Revelation 22:16 – *"I Jesus have sent mine angel to testify unto you these things in the **churches**. I am the root and the offspring of David, and the bright and morning star."*

APPENDIX C

The word **assembly (ekklesia)** in the New Testament

Acts 19:32 – *"Some therefore cried one thing, and some another: for the **assembly** was confused; and the more part knew not wherefore they were come together."*

Acts 19:39 – *"But if ye inquire anything concerning other matters, it shall be determined in a lawful **assembly**."*

Acts 19:41 – *"And when he had thus spoken, he dismissed the **assembly**."*

APPENDIX D

NOTE ON ACTS 7:38

Although Stephen is speaking of the assembled Israelites, and in no way is even remotely referring to the New Testament Church, we do learn that the word **Ekklesia** that is used here refers to a definite literal group of people in a specific geographical location.

APPENDIX E

THE FOOLISHNESS OF SEEKING TO DO THE LORD'S WORK APART FROM THE HOLY SPIRIT!

The Comforter has come, The Comforter
  has come!
The Holy Ghost from heav'n, the Father's promise
  giv'n;
O spread the tidings 'round, wherever man
  is found
The Comforter has come!
                 – C. Austin Miles

DURING OLD TESTAMENT TIMES WHEN GOD HAD A JOB FOR SOMEONE TO DO THE HOLY SPIRIT ENABLED THEM TO DO IT

In the Book of Exodus, we learn it was God's will for the Tabernacle to be built. Exodus 31:1-3, reveals that **the Holy Spirit** enabled Bezaleel and others to accomplish this special task. In Judges 3:9-11, it was God's will for the Israelites to be delivered from bondage; **the Holy Spirit** enabled Othniel to lead the people to victory. Judges 6:34, reveals it was God's will for the Israelites to be delivered from the hands of the Midianites. **The Holy Spirit** enabled Gideon to lead the people on to victory in a battle that from the human standpoint they should have never won. We discover in Judges 14:6, 19; 15:14, that Samson's amazing strength was the result of **the Holy Spirit** being upon him. In I Samuel 16:13, David needed divine enablement as King; therefore, **The Spirit of the Lord** came upon him. In Zechariah 4:6, 7, we have the wonderful statement: *"Then he answered and spake unto me, saying, Not by might, nor by power, but by my spirit saith the Lord of hosts. Who art thou, O great mountain? before Zerbbabel thou shalt become a plain . . ."* **The Holy Spirit** can give victory in times of utter human impossibility!

THE MINISTRY OF OUR BLESSED MASTER WAS PERFORMED UNDER THE CONTROL OF THE HOLY SPIRIT

Our blessed Master was: **filled** with the Holy Spirit (Luke 4:1);

131

led by the Holy Spirit (Luke 4:1); the Spirit was **upon** Him (Luke 4:18); **empowered** by the Holy Spirit (Luke 4:14, Matthew 12:28); and according to Acts 10:38, He was **anointed** with the Holy Spirit.

THE DISCIPLES WERE NOT TO BEGIN THE WORK OF LOCAL OR WORLD EVANGELIZATION UNTIL THEY WERE FILLED WITH THE HOLY SPIRIT

Luke 24:49 – *". . . but tarry ye in the city of Jerusalem UNTIL ye be endued with* **POWER FROM ON HIGH.** *"*

The Lord went up, the Spirit came down, and the church went out in the book of Acts. Christ is the theme; the church is the means; and the Spirit is the power!

Acts 1:8 – *"But ye shall receive* **power***, AFTER that the Holy Spirit is come upon you: and ye shall be witnesses unto me . . ."*

THE LOCAL NEW TESTAMENT CHURCH CARRIED ON GOD'S WORK IN THE POWER OF THE HOLY SPIRIT

There are seven specific times in the Book of Acts when the early believers are said to be filled with the Holy Spirit. A study of these verses is crucial and essential.

1. they were filled to witness (Acts 2:4; 4:8, 31)
2. they were filled to serve (Acts 6:3)
3. they were filled to edify (Acts 11:24)
4. they were filled to rebuke (Acts 13:9)
5. they were filled as they were dying (Acts 7:55)

EPHESIANS 5:18 IS A DIVINE IMPERATIVE FOR ALL BELIEVERS TODAY

It is God's will for every member of every local church to be constantly filled with the Holy Spirit at all times. Ephesians 5:18 is for everyone. *"Be filled with the Spirit."* **First**, the verb **PLEROUSTHE** is in the imperative mood. That simply means it is a command. We are commanded to be filled with the Holy Spirit. We are never commanded to be baptized, sealed, or indwelt by the Holy Spirit. These things are positional; they refer to something God does for us as writing our names in the Book of Life. The command to be filled with the Holy Spirit relates not to our position before God, but to our daily service and walk. **Second**, the tense of this verb **PLEROUSTHE** is the present tense. "Tense" to us in the English language means "time." But what we call "tense" in Greek verbs is not "tense" at all. Greek verbs express kinds of action, as a point (aorist), continuous as going on (present), having been completed and remaining completed (perfect), etc. This verb is in the present tense and refers to enduring, continuous action. It is God's will for all of His children to be constantly filled with the Holy Spirit. **Third**, the verb **PLEROUSTHE** is in the plural number. This teaches us that this command is addressed, not only to the preacher, the deacon, the Sunday School teacher, but to every Christian and to every church member. It is the responsibility of every believer to always be filled with the Holy Spirit. **Fourth**, the verb **PLEROUSTHE** is in the passive voice. The subject is acted upon. The filling of the Spirit is not a work of man, but of God. He will fill us and make definite changes in our lives for His glory. The evidence of this will be obvious (Galatians 5:22, 23).

To be filled with and constantly controlled by the Holy Spirit is the norm for all believers today.

THE GREAT TRAGEDY

The tragedy is that many times we are seeking to do the Lord's work apart from the Holy Spirit. It is so easy to depend more upon personalities, programs, and human persuasiveness than the Holy Spirit. According to Acts 13:4, 3, and 2, the New Testament Church was in complete cooperation with the Holy Spirit. Often, we don't even take the Holy Spirit into our plans and considerations.

Frequently, we don't have power in our walk and witness because we have allowed sin to grieve, quench, and stifle the Holy Spirit's work in our lives. Commonly, we live totally apart from the fullness of the Holy Spirit and, we must admit, a great deal of God's work is carried on in the energy of the flesh totally apart from the Holy Spirit.

The story is told of the man, who was a little hard of hearing, vacuuming the church auditorium. While vacuuming the auditorium, the plug from the vacuum cleaner came out of the outlet. However, the man just kept on carefully and, he thought, thoroughly, vacuuming the auditorium for quite some time. As time passed, someone walked into the auditorium and told the man that the vacuum cleaner was unplugged. To his surprise, he finally realized that although working painstakingly and attentively, he had not accomplished anything because the vacuum cleaner was not plugged in. We could say, that often we seek to do the **Lord's** work without being empowered by the Holy Spirit. Have we been depending more upon self than the Holy Spirit? Have we been living apart from the Holy Spirit's power in our lives? It is absolutely necessary to be completely emptied of self in order to be filled with the Holy Spirit. None of self and all of Thee: *". . . not I, but Christ . . ."* (Galatians 2:20).

> I am weakness, full of weakness,
> At Thy sacred feet I bow;
> Blest, divine eternal Spirit,
> Fill with pow'r, and fill me now.
> – Elwood R. Stokes

APPENDIX F

1. A Saved Church – *"which delivered us from the wrath to come"* (1:10d)

2. A Sound Church – *"having received the word"* (1:6b)

3. A Suffering Church – *"in much affliction"* (1:6c)

4. A Soul-Winning Church – *"for from you sounded out the word of the Lord"* (1:8)

5. A Separated Church – *"how ye turned to God from idols"* (1:9b)

6. A Serving Church – *"to serve the living and true God"* (1:9c)

7. A Second Coming Church – *"and to wait for his Son from heaven"* (1:10a)

APPENDIX G

"The Church According To"
I Thessalonians

1. A Center for Evangelism (1:8)

2. A Nursery for Spiritual Babes (2:7, 8)

3. A Family Where Love Prevails (3:12; 4:9, 10)

4. A School for Character Development (4:3-12)

5. A Place of Divine Correction (5:14a, 4:11, 12)

6. A Hospital for the Spiritually Weak (5:14b)

7. A Target for the Devil (2:14, 15; 2:18; 3:5)

APPENDIX H

"THE CHURCH AT ANTIOCH"
ACTS 13:1-4

1. A Diversified Church (13:1)
   a. Barnabas (from Cyprus an island 60 miles off the coast of Syria)
   b. Simeon called Niger (an African?)
   c. Lucius of Cyrene (Cyrene, North Africa – located in modern-day Libya)
   d. Manaen (brought up with the well known Herod of the Gospels, Matthew 14:1-10; Mark. 8:15; Luke 8:3)
   e. Saul (from Tarsus, located in modern-day Turkey)

2. A Teaching Church (13:1)

3. A Praying Church (13:1)

4. A Fasting Church (13:2, 3)

5. A Holy Spirit Directed Church (13:4, 3, 2)

6. A Reproducing Church (13:3-4, 49; 14:1, 7, 21-23, 27)

APPENDIX I

"The Church At Smyrna: The Faithful, Rewarded Church"
What A Church!
Revelation 2:8-11

1. The Church (vs. 8a)
   a. The pastor
   b. The place

2. The Christ (vs. 8b)
   a. The First and the Last
   b. The One Who was dead and is alive

3. The Condemnation (none!) What a church!

4. The Commendation (vs. 9)
   a. of their works (vs. 9a)
   b. of their tribulation (vs. 9b, d)
   c. of their poverty (vs. 9c)

5. The Counsel (vs. 10)
   a. fear not (vs. 10a, b)
   b. be faithful (vs. 10c)

6. The Compensation (vs. 10d, 11b)
   a. I will give thee a crown of life (vs. 10d)
   b. You will not be hurt of the second death (vs. 11b)

7. The Call (vs. 11a)

APPENDIX J

The Secret

I met God in the morning,
When the day was at its best.
And His presence came like sunrise,
Like a glory in my breast.

All day long the presence lingered,
All day long He stayed with me.
And we sailed in perfect calmness,
Over a very troubled sea.

Other ships were blown and battered,
Other ships were sore distressed,
But the winds that seemed to drive them,
Brought to me a peace and rest.

Then I thought of other mornings,
With a keen remorse of mind.
When I too had loosed the moorings,
With the presence left behind.

So I think I know the secret,
Learned from many a troubled way.
You must seek Him in the morning,
If you want Him thru the day.

– Ralph Cushman

APPENDIX K

SPURGEON ON THE LESS THAN PERFECT CHURCH

One day someone approached Charles Haddon Spurgeon, the renowned British Baptist pastor. Spurgeon inquired why the gentleman had not united with the church. The man responded, "I started to join the church, but I looked around, and I saw a hypocrite. I decided not to join."

Spurgeon replied: "In the first church, the leader Peter cursed; Thomas doubted the resurrection; Judas, the treasurer, betrayed the Lord. The first church was not perfect! Furthermore, I have never seen a church that is perfect. But, sir, if you ever find the perfect church, please do not join, for when you become a member, it will no longer be perfect."

NOTES

(The quoted material in this book is not a blanket endorsement of all the works cited.)

CHAPTER II
NEW TESTAMENT CHURCH MEMBERS WERE BAPTIZED

[1] James Orr, ed., The International Standard Bible Encyclopedia (Grand Rapids, Mich.: Wm. B. Eerdmans Publishing Co., 1960), vol. I, 386. Also, Harold L. Fichett, Jr., A Layman's Guide To Baptist Beliefs (Grand Rapids, Mich.: Zondervan Publishing House, 1975), 72.

[2] Charles C. Ryrie, Basic Theology (Wheaton, Ill.: Victor Books, 1990) "Immersion is unquestionably the primary meaning of **Baptizo.** The Greek language has words for sprinkle and pour which are never used of baptism.", 424.

[3] John Calvin, Institutes of the Christian Religion, 5th ed. translated by John Allen. 2 volumes. (Philadelphia, Pa.: Presbyterian Board of Publication and Sabbath School Work, 1902), 522-524. Calvin also affirms immersion in his comment on Acts 8:38 Commentary Upon the Acts of the Apostles, 2 volumes (Edinburgh: Calvin Translation Society, 1844).

[4] Wace and Buchheim, ed., Luther's Primary Works (London: Hodder and Stoughton, 1896), 347.

[5] Wesley states this in his Notes Upon the New Testament in commenting on Romans 6:4.

CHAPTER VII
NEW TESTAMENT CHURCH MEMBERS WERE UNDERSTANDING

[1] Matthew Henry, Commentary on the Whole Bible (New York: Fleming H. Revell Co.), volume VI, 708.

[2] R. C. Lenski, I and II Corinthians (Minneapolis: Augsburg Publishing House, 1963), 245.

Chapter IX
New Testament Church Members Were Soul Winners
(every member evangelism)

[1] George Verwer, Come! Live! Die! (Wheaton, Ill.: Tyndale, 1972), 95-96.

Chapter XIII
God's Only Program For Planet Earth

[1] G. H. Lang, The Churches of God (London: Paternoster Press, n. d.), 11.

[2] Ibid., 11.

[3] D. B. Eastep, Highway Robbery from the Scriptural Standpoint (Covington, Ky.: Calvary Book Room, n. d.).

[4] Warren W. Wiersbe, Expository Outlines on the New Testament (Covington, Ky.: Calvary Baptist Church Book Room, 1966) II Corinthians 8:1 (not to be reprinted, quotation used by permission).

Chapter XIV
New Testament Church Members Were Identified

[1] James Bannerman, The Church of Christ (Banner of Truth, 1960), chapter 2 of volume 1.

[2] Ernest D. Pickering, What Church Should You Join? (Tract).

[3] Gene A. Getz, Sharpening the Focus of the Church (Chicago: Moody Press, 1977), 47.

[4] W. Carlton Long, unpublished notes.

[5] John R. Rice, Seven Secrets of a Happy, Prosperous Christian Life (Murfreesboro, Tn.: Sword of the Lord, 1966), 27-31.

[6] R. A. Torrey, How to Succeed in the Christian Life (Chicago: Moody Press, 1907), 41-42.

Chapter XV
New Testament Church Members Were Faithful

[1] Charles C. Ryrie, Basic Theology (Wheaton, Ill.: Victor Books, 1990), 394. "Nevertheless, the word as used in the

New Testament still retains **the basic meaning of an assembly**, and does not take on a supposed theological meaning (based on the breakup of the word into its two parts, 'call' and 'out of') of a 'called out' people. If the word is going to be translated on the basis of etymology, then it should be translated 'called together,' not 'called out.'"

CHAPTER XVI
NEW TESTAMENT CHURCH MEMBERS WERE GENEROUS

[1] F. B. Meyer, <u>Abraham God's Friend</u> (Westchester, Ill.: Good News Publishers, 1962), 29.

[2] George H. E. Salstrand, <u>The Tithe</u>, 52-53.

[3] <u>Bill Gothard</u>: "We believe that the tithe is the minimum that should be given . . ." article, <u>The Tithe</u> (How to Manage Your Money Newsletter – August 15, 1990 – Christian Financial Concepts). <u>Howard Hendricks</u>: "I would take the tithe as a starting point. I think that often you get the reactionary type of mentality that says, 'Well, I'm under grace and there's no need.' While I would say it's not a legal requirement, it certainly is a standard pattern." article, <u>The Tithe</u> (How to Manage Your Money Newsletter – August 15, 1990 – Christian Financial Concepts). <u>Larry Burkett</u>: "one of the first standards of giving found in the Bible is the tithe, a word which means 'tenth.' Abraham tithed in Genesis 14 after returning from the daring rescue of his nephew Lot from four enemy kings. He encountered the priest Melchizedek and voluntarily surrendered to him one tenth of all the spoils he had taken from his enemies. It's often said that the tithe is Old Testament 'legalism,' but, Abraham tithed some 430 years before the Law was given to Moses." booklet, <u>Giving and Tithing</u>, (Christian Financial Concepts: Gainsville, Ga., 1992), 3. (Quoting these men is not an endorsement of their ministries. They are simply cited to indicate that some who are **not** strong local church men and are **not** pastors hold to the position that the tithe should be the beginning point of Christian giving.)

[4] <u>Warren W. Wiersbe</u>: "Giving was church-centered." <u>Wiersbe's Expository Outlines on the New Testament</u>

(Wheaton, Ill.: Victory Books, 1992), 468. <u>Gothard</u>: "It is our understanding from Scripture that the tithe should be directed to or through the local church." (How to Manage Your Money Newsletter – August 15, 1990 – Christian Financial Concepts – article <u>The Tithe</u>). <u>Burkett</u>: "You can't sit under the teaching of a local church and not support it financially." He indicates that if the local church is doing its job, then your tithes should be directed to or through the local church. Article <u>The Tithe</u> (How to Manage Your Money Newsletter – August 15, 1990).

These men, along with many others, teach that a believer **ideally** should give to and through his local church. Commonly, they teach that the church should come first in the Christian's giving. However, they also clearly and forthrightly teach that a believer **should not give exclusively** to or through one's local church. Therefore, **leaving the door open** to a lot of unscriptural giving **outside** the local church. The result is an explosion and proliferation of "Ministries" (Christian organizations and parachurch groups, etc.) outside the local church.

These men, and many others, make a **common and accepted mistake**. They see the importance of the local church: However, they fail to see the **centrality** and **primacy** of the local church. Most people who study the New Testament see the importance of the church because it cannot be avoided: It is clearly obvious. However, few see, or want to see, the truth of local church **centrality** and **primacy**. Many talk about its importance; **but fail to emphasize its centrality and primacy**. Not everyone who says he is local church is, in reality and actuality, **local church in practice**.

The New Testament, not only teaches the importance of the church, but also, the **centrality** of the church in the work of the Lord.

New Testament giving is local church giving **period**. No other type giving is even hinted at in the New Testament.

About The Author

Jim Gent has spent the last twenty-nine years in local church planting, pastoring, and evangelism. He is currently the pastor of the Garden State Baptist Church of Old Bridge, New Jersey, of which he is also the founder. He is a graduate of Tennessee Temple College and Temple Baptist Theological Seminary.